QUENCH

Quench

HANDCRAFTED BEVERAGES TO
SATISFY EVERY TASTE & OCCASION

Ashley English

Photographs by Jen Altman

ROOST BOOKS
Boston & London 2014

ROOST BOOKS
An imprint of Shambhala Publications, Inc.
Horticultural Hall
300 Massachusetts Avenue
Boston, Massachusetts 02115
roostbooks.com

9 8 7 6 5 4 3 2 1

First Edition
Printed in the United States of America

∞ This edition is printed on acid-free paper that meets the American National Standards Institute z39.48 Standard.
♲ Shambhala makes every effort to print on recycled paper.
For more information please visit www.shambhala.com.

Distributed in the United States by Penguin Random House LLC and in Canada by Random House of Canada Ltd

Designed by Daniel Urban-Brown

LIBRARY OF CONGRESS CATALOGING-IN-PUBLICATION DATA

English, Ashley, 1976–
Quench: handcrafted beverages to satisfy every taste and occasion / Ashley English.
Pages   cm
Includes index.
ISBN 978-1-61180-128-6 (alk. paper)
1. Beverages. I. Title.
TX815.E55 2014
641.2—dc23
2013038831

To Mom and Dad, who never let me go thirsty.

contents

introduction

There are many things that we, as humans, can live without. Cars, computers, even electricity—all luxuries when it comes to our continued survival, albeit ones we've come to depend on rather heavily. One thing we can't do without, though, that we simply cannot continue with the prolonged absence of, is water. Our bodies are composed of it and require a daily supply and renewal of this life-giving fluid in order to both thrive and survive. We thirst and must have that thirst quenched, with regularity, to go about our lives, enjoying all the other lovely aspects of being alive.

Which is where this book comes into play. Yes, we must drink, and drink daily, to have our needs met, to actually live our lives. While water in its unadorned form is glorious, giving it a flavor injection or otherwise doctoring it up a bit makes meeting this most basic of needs considerably more pleasurable and palatable. From creamy milks to juicy fruits, flavorful sodas, and healthful teas, beverages attend to our liquid requirements while satisfying body and soul alike. Cocktails, punches, and other boozy options, meanwhile, imbue a festive and celebratory note to our gatherings and occasions. Let's drink, and drink deeply and satisfyingly.

Of course, at this time in history it's easy to walk into a grocery store or stop by a coffee shop for a delicious beverage. Why then take the time to create them yourself instead? I've given this question a good deal of rumination over the years, especially when writing this book (and making the recipes here many times over). Here's what I've decided upon:

HOMEMADE BEVERAGES ARE HEALTHIER. When you've made a drink yourself, you know precisely what is and is not in it. In with all-natural ingredients; out with additives, preservatives, stabilizers, fixatives, and artificial ingredients in general. This is the single largest motivator for me when it comes to creating beverages at home.

HOMEMADE BEVERAGES ARE PERSONAL. The drinks you make are infinitely customizable. Craft them to fit your own flavor interests. You're the mixologist at the helm of this liquid ship, so shape that drink the way you want it to be! When you purchase prepared goods, you're at the mercy of whatever offerings manufacturers have created.

HOMEMADE BEVERAGES OFTEN COST LESS. Hidden costs lurk in all prepared food items, and often for good reason. There's the cost to cover producing the drink, labeling it, shipping it, advertising it, storing it, and then reselling it on a retail level. All along the way, costs are incurred in the end beverage product. Making a beverage in your own kitchen, using simple, basic, fresh ingredients, cuts the costs considerably. Aside from paying for ingredients and, where necessary, equipment, and perhaps the modest costs produced by storing your drink in the refrigerator (which is likely already in use anyway), there's no other debt incurred in creating beverages at home.

HOMEMADE BEVERAGES PRODUCE LESS WASTE. I am a waste-reducing vigilante. Whenever an item can be reused, recycled, or otherwise repurposed, I'm all over it. The packaging and raw materials used in generating commercially produced beverages are often tossed out. At home, you're able to continually reuse the materials that house your beverages, as well as compost spent ingredients. The ability to cut down on the waste stream is therefore significant.

HOMEMADE BEVERAGES OFTEN TASTE BETTER. Have you ever had a glass of homemade eggnog before? I'd say it's safe to call such a drink "transcendent" without being hyperbolic. Do a side-by-side comparison of your homemade creamy concoction with a quart purchased in the dairy aisle, and you'll immediately understand why going the distance in your own kitchen is so very worthwhile. That's just one example. Beverages made at home and then quickly consumed offer the potential for exemplary flavor that simply can't be achieved by one that has sat upon store shelves for some time.

In the pages of *Quench*, you'll find a beverage for every need, a flavor for every palate. Whether you're looking for a means of making kombucha at home, a stellar recipe for brewing a warm mug of homemade chai, help with crafting your own Limoncello, or simply tips for creating boozy punches perfect for parties, you'll find a bevy of beverage delights for wetting your whistle and quenching your thirst. I've also included suggestions for selecting ingredients and equipment that will encourage your adventures in beverage making to go as smoothly and seamlessly as possible.

I'm a big proponent of community building and resource sharing. If there's a mu-

tually beneficial way to include friends, family, and the greater community in a project I've devised, I'll likely do so. Here, that's evidenced by the inclusion of a number of recipes from guest contributors. Whether real-world, longtime friends like my buddy Trevor Baker, proprietor of Noble Cider, who's sharing his recipe for homemade Hard Cider (page 174), or digital ones like my professional and personal relationship with Marisa McClellan, blogger and author of *Food in Jars,* who's offering her recipe for a Blood Orange Shrub (page 35), I've hooked my wagon to those of several other fans of handmade beverage crafting.

Alongside go-to recipes I've created over the years, I've shared a series of beverage trips down memory lane in this book. Certain drinks have a lasting resonance, a lingering significance that persists long after the glass has been drained of its contents. Sprinkled throughout the pages of *Quench*, you'll learn why I'll always associate pear nectar with working in a bakery my freshman year of college, why hot chocolate instantly transports me to the heady days of love and romance and Paris during my honeymoon, and why mulled wine will forever in my mind be linked to a group of sugar-fueled, raucous women.

With *Quench*, my hope is to introduce you to handcrafted beverages with a refrigerator and cocktail cabinet's worth of offerings and clear, straightforward instructions and suggestions. If you're already onboard with home beverage making, there's plenty in these pages for you, too. Whatever brought you here, I promise you won't leave parched. Cheers!

ingredients and equipment

You know you want to craft homemade beverages; all you need now are the tools of the trade. In this chapter we'll examine some of the ingredients and equipment necessary to create a bevy of liquid delights!

Ingredients

Crafting a delicious homemade beverage is really all about the ingredients. Starting out with quality goods sets the stage for building a stellar drink. You're going to the trouble to make your own beverages, after all, so get a strong foothold right out of the gate by selecting the best items you can find within your budget. Here I've provided a few specific notes on some of the ingredients called for in this book.

Chocolate and coffee

When making any beverage with chocolate or coffee included, I like to use selections labeled fair-trade. Fair-trade is a social movement and system of exchange that considers all aspects of a commodity's production, including its producers, consumers, communities, and environment. Fair-trade organizations and businesses promote practices such as a living wage for employees, safe working conditions, a fair exchange rate for the goods produced, and consideration of local communities and environments. In particular, fair-trade focuses on exports from so-called developing nations to "developed" countries and involves commodities such as handicrafts, coffee, chocolate, bananas, sugar, tea, and wine. It's fairly easy to find fair-trade ingredients these days at both large chain grocery stores and small natural foods stores alike.

Dairy

All of the dairy items used in recipe development for this book are full-fat products, including buttermilk, half-and-half, heavy cream, milk, and yogurt. Many sessions of trial and error have made me a firm believer that full-fat options yield the best flavor and texture. I also use all organic dairy products, and often seek out those produced by small creameries, in order to support both organic agriculture and small family farms. Furthermore, dairy products from organic dairies are free of antibiotics, artificial growth hormones, genetically modified organisms (GMOs), irradiation, and sewage waste—all good things to avoid in my estimation.

Eggs

All of the eggs used in this book are large eggs. My eggs come from my own free-range, organically fed chickens. If such eggs are available to you, I encourage you to opt for them. Both the flavor and nutrient profile offered by eggs sourced from free-range chickens far surpass those of conventionally produced eggs.

Herbs

A number of the recipes found here call for the use of fresh herbs. I attempt to use fresh herbs, as opposed to dry, whenever possible. That said, if you cannot find a source of fresh herbs, feel free to substitute dried, using half the amount called for. Herbs called for in some of the recipes, however, should only be used in dried form. This is the case with a number of the medicinal herbs used in the bitters recipes. When an herb should specifically be incorporated in such a format, the recipe will indicate as much. Some of the more difficult-to-find herbs can be sourced online (see *Resources,* page 194).

Pantry goods

For pantry items such as nuts and rice, seek out the freshest options available. If you don't often use these ingredients and worry about any unused portion going bad, I suggest visiting a grocery or natural foods store with bulk bins and purchasing only as much as you'll need at a time. Well-trafficked stores with a high turnover of bulk bin goods will have the freshest selection. Whenever flavor extracts are called for here, including vanilla, orange, almond, and peppermint, you'll want to use all-natural, real

extracts. Imitation extracts not only are full of synthetic flavor agents and preservatives; they also lack the powerful flavor available in authentic extracts and won't offer your homemade beverages their due justice.

Produce

When selecting fruits and vegetables for your beverages, seek out the freshest, ripest fruits and vegetables you can find. Look for bruise- and blemish-free offerings, if at all possible. Farmer's markets and orchards are wonderful sources of fresh, seasonal produce. You can also just make friends with the produce manager wherever you shop and inquire what days the produce deliveries are made to ensure access to the best specimens.

Spices

Though we sometimes don't think of it, spices, like all foodstuffs, have a shelf life. Give an annual look at the expiration dates on your spice jars. Choose a date you're unlikely to forget, such as New Year's Day, or your birthday or anniversary. Anything older than a year old should be composted. If you worry you won't use a full bottle of a given spice in a year, try to find a store that sells spices in bulk and purchase smaller quantities you're likely to go through quickly.

Sugars

Unless otherwise indicated, the sugar called for in a recipe is granulated cane sugar. Light and dark brown sugars are specifically indicated accordingly. The difference in color between light and dark brown sugar owes to the amount of molasses each contains, with dark brown sugar containing a higher percentage. Where alternative sweeteners are called for, such as honey or Turbinado sugar, the recipe will specifically indicate their use.

Wine yeast

Several of the recipes in the Warming and Fermented chapter call for wine or cider-making yeasts. Such items can be sourced at a homebrew supply store or online (see *Resources,* page 194).

Equipment

While most of the equipment needed to craft beverages at home likely already lives in your kitchen, several recipes require the use of special items.

Food processor or blender

These two kitchen workhorses come in quite handy when making beverages. From pureeing fruit for nectars to breaking down watermelon for agua frescas and simply blitzing milkshakes, having a high-quality food processor or a blender on hand is suggested.

Glass bottles

An array of bottles is essential in making beverages here. You'll need them not only for the infusing and ageing process but also for later, to store your finished liquids in. Canisters with flip- or screw-top lids can be quite helpful during the infusing stage. For storage, I try to keep a selection of empty bottles on hand at all times, upcycling those formerly housing liquor, olive oil, maple syrup, vinegar, and other commercially purchased items.

Wine and cider equipment

The recipes for wine and cider making each include some suggestions for materials specific to those particular types of beverage. Siphons, carboys, hydrometers, rubber stoppers, airlocks, fermenting crocks, and more are listed as "equipment" in recipes indicating their requirement. Such items can be found locally, if you have a homebrew or homesteading supply store, or online at brewing suppliers.

Cheesecloth

Many recipes call for the use of cheesecloth for filtering out solids. When it is called for, be sure to choose a finely woven cheesecloth with a high thread count, not the flimsy, low-quality offering found at grocery stores. Butter muslin can also be used. Such items can be found at good kitchen stores and homesteading supply stores, as well as online.

Muslin tea bags

Several recipes call for muslin tea bags for infusing herbs and spices in larger amounts of liquid. This type of bag is made of a finely woven cotton cloth with a drawstring top. Some grocery and natural foods stores carry them in their bulk tea, herb, and spice aisles. Otherwise, they can be easily sourced online.

Fine-mesh sieve

The straining off of solid ingredients is called for in numerous recipes in this book. In order to effectively do so, you'll need to employ a fine-mesh sieve. These sieves are easily found in kitchen supply stores or kitchen tool areas of large retail stores. They can also be purchased online.

Punch bowls

While a punch bowl may seem like an antiquated artifact, come party time, it'll get a good deal of use. Many can be found at thrift stores and garage sales, as well as purchased new. My punch bowl does double duty, transforming from a cake stand with a domed glass lid into a party bowl when inverted.

Lidded storage pitchers

Many of these beverages need to be stored in the refrigerator once completed—if they're not completely consumed straightaway. To keep odors and aromas out and your liquid contents in, you'll want to store them in lidded containers or pitchers. I like to use glass pitchers with handles and lids designed expressly for fitting in refrigerator doors.

Other essentials

Various-sized sharp kitchen knives, colander, cutting board, mixing bowls, stainless-steel pots and pans with lids, liquid measuring cups, measuring spoons, dry measuring cups, whisk, wooden spoons.

SOFT DRINKS

———————— ❧ ————————

SODAS, JUICES, MILKS (AND THEIR SHAKES!), TEAS, COFFEES—THESE ARE THE GENTLE, SOOTHING, SATISFYING BEVERAGES THAT MAKE UP THE CATEGORY COLLECTIVELY REFERRED TO AS "SOFT" DRINKS. FROM A COLD, CRISP, SPARKLING ORANGE SODA TO A WARMING MUG OF CHAI, THE RECIPES IN THIS SECTION COVER THE SPECTRUM OF BEVERAGE NEEDS, WANTS, DESIRES, AND AGES. WEE ONES TO THE SENIOR SET CAN IMBIBE ALIKE WITHIN THESE PAGES. I HOPE THESE RECIPES SERVE AS A CATALYST OF INSPIRATION, TOO, INVITING YOU TO FILL THE FRIDGE AND PANTRY WITH QUENCHING CONCOCTIONS OF YOUR OWN.

refreshing

Some days, all it takes is a cool, zippy drink to cure whatever ails you. The beverages found in this section are intended for that very thing. Puckery lemonades, bubbly sodas, sweet nectars, and jazzed-up waters—they're all here, ready, willing, and able to make your mouth (and your attitude) happy.

Lavender Lemonade

makes 1 gallon

14 cups cold water, divided

1½ to 2 cups sugar (depending on desired sweetness)

2 tablespoons lavender buds (fresh or dried)

1⅔ cups fresh lemon juice (from about 6 to 8 lemons, depending on size)

Ice, to serve

There is a lavender, goat, and blueberry farm about an hour north from us, located in the small mountain town of Burnsville, North Carolina. Each June, around Father's Day weekend, Mountain Farm opens its doors to the public for their Lavender Festival. Along with a lavender labyrinth to walk, baby goats to pet, and epic mountain views to admire, there is an abundance of lavender-infused food and drink to enjoy at the festival. The farm's lavender lemonade inspired this recipe. Take care to follow the recipe precisely, as infusing the lavender longer than indicated takes the flavor of the flowers from pleasant and subtle to medicinal and overpowering.

Combine 4 cups of water, sugar, and lavender buds in a medium-size saucepan. Bring to a gentle boil, and simmer for 5 minutes. Remove the saucepan from the heat, and strain the syrup through a fine-mesh sieve. Compost the solids.

Combine the lavender syrup with 10 cups of cold water and the lemon juice. Stir to fully blend. Store in the refrigerator in a lidded container. Serve in individual glasses with ice.

Ginger Lemonade

I was pregnant with my son Huxley during what turned out to be the hottest summer in western North Carolina in fifty years. We lived in a 1930s bungalow without air-conditioning. Owing to those factors, and to my extra girth, I became possessed of a nearly insatiable thirst and a constant elevated temperature. My sweet husband, Glenn, whipped up a pitcher of this lemonade one particularly warm day to tend to his otherwise pleasant (but increasingly miserable) spouse. The ginger's warmth paired perfectly with the acidity of the lemon and cut through the sweetness. My thirst was quenched, and our union remained intact!

Combine 4 cups of water and the sugar in a small saucepan. Heat until just boiling, stirring until the sugar granules completely dissolve. Remove the pan from the heat, and whisk in the honey. Add the ginger, cover the pan, and steep for 10 minutes.

Strain the syrup through a fine-mesh sieve placed atop a 1-gallon pitcher to remove the ginger. Compost the solids.

Add the lemon juice to the pitcher. Fill with the remaining 10 cups of cold water. Top off with ice cubes. Stir to combine. Store the pitcher in the refrigerator until ready to serve. Serve in individual glasses with a little curl of lemon peel garnish, if desired.

makes 1 gallon

14 cups cold water, divided

¾ cup sugar

¼ cup honey

1 tablespoon minced fresh ginger

Juice and pulp from 5 or 6 lemons (with the seeds strained out; about 1¼–1½ cups juice)

Ice

Lemon peel, for garnish (optional)

Blueberry Lemonade

makes 1 gallon

Simple syrup (recipe follows)

1¾ cups blueberries, divided

Juice and pulp from 6 large
    lemons (with the seeds
    strained out; about 1½
    cups juice)

Cold water

Ice

For the Simple Syrup

1 cup boiling water

¾ cup sugar

¼ cup honey

I have a long history with blueberries. My grandmother owned a pick-your-own blueberry farm when I was a child, and today my husband and I have our own "Blueberry Hill" at our home, planted with seventeen bushes. To top it off, our son resembles the title character in Robert Mc-Closkey's Caldecott Medal–winning children's book, Blueberries for Sal, *which he loves dearly. It's understandable, therefore, that the indigo-hued orbs would make their way into a pitcher of lemonade for me. On one of the dog days of summer, when simply remaining upright feels like too much work, pour a glass of this lemonade, find a shady spot (or better yet, a hammock!), and sip the swelter away.*

Combine the boiling water, sugar, and honey in a heatproof bowl to make a simple syrup. Whisk until the ingredients are fully incorporated. Allow to cool slightly, about 5 minutes.

Puree 1½ cups of blueberries in a food processor or blender until smooth. Add the simple syrup, and process until fully blended. Strain the blueberry syrup through a fine-mesh sieve placed atop a 1-gallon pitcher. Using a spoon, gently press the solids, forcing out as much liquid as possible. Compost the solids.

Add the lemon juice to the pitcher. Fill ¾ full with ice-cold water. Top off with ice cubes and ¼ cup of blueberries. Stir to combine. Store the pitcher in the refrigerator until ready to serve.

QUENCHED: LEMONADE

My father has seven brothers and sisters. Each of those siblings, in turn, has at least one child, though most have closer to three or four. Growing up in the Philadelphia/South New Jersey area as they did meant hot, humid summers, best spent surfside on the coast just a short drive away. Avalon, New Jersey, was the family's chosen summer destination. Each year, for a week or two, a large house would be rented. Aunts, uncles, cousins, and grandparents would descend for scorching days lounging on the beach (or, for the little set, building and repeatedly destroying sandcastles). Evenings were characterized by epic feasts involving Silver Queen corn and scandalously ripe tomatoes followed by Skee-Ball sessions and fudge- and salt water taffy–fueled adventures on the boardwalk.

A creature of habit and order for as long as I can recall, each day I'd pack myself a lunch and head to the "shore," to use the common parlance, with some family member. Without fail, this lunch consisted of several Oreo cookies, a turkey or ham sandwich, and an insulated thermos full of instant lemonade. Lemonade was my thirst quencher during those Jersey shore days, as the salt water found its way into every individual shaft of hair on my head and sand infiltrated not just my clothing but my toys, gear, and, yes, sometimes even my lunch. Lemonade hit the spot, to be sure, and wetted my parched whistle.

The family still gathers at the shore each summer, but in a different town now. My grandparents have passed away, cousins have married and begun families of their own, and my harried schedule and southern location make it difficult to join the rendezvous. No matter, though. Whenever I sip on a cold glass of lemonade (freshly squeezed now, thank you kindly), I'm back on the beach, munching on my lunch, chatting with my extended tribe, and enjoying the carefree days of childhood.

Orangeade

I will forever associate orangeade with my earliest memories of Disney World. I can acutely recall waiting in long lines in the punishing Orlando sun, experiencing for the first time the simultaneous thrill and terror of riding Space Mountain, and, the saving grace, consuming copious glasses of ice-cold orangeade. That holy trinity of fresh orange juice, sugar, and ice made everything in the Magic Kingdom infinitely better. I wish the very same childlike happiness for you here. Consuming a glass of this orangeade via a swirly straw is optional but highly encouraged.

Combine 4 cups of water and the sugar in a medium-size saucepan. Bring to a boil, stirring until the sugar granules are completely dissolved. Simmer for 5 minutes. Remove the saucepan from the heat.

Add 3 cups of cold water, orange juice, and lemon juice. Stir to fully combine. Store in a lidded container in the refrigerator. Serve in individual glasses with ice.

makes ½ gallon

7 cups cold water, divided

¾ cup sugar

1 cup fresh orange juice

2 tablespoons fresh lemon juice

Ice, to serve

Limeade

For a brief one and a half years, I had the exquisite pleasure of living on the panhandle of Florida in the sensational seaside town of Destin. On Sunday afternoons, my mother, brother, and I would head a few miles down the road to the tiny hamlet of Grayton Beach. In a small, unassuming café, we'd order soft-shell crab sandwiches and slices of Key lime pie. Whenever I sip this limeade, I'm transported back to those days when salty air permeated everything (including my adolescent hair), bathing suits were considered acceptable dining attire, and the food was served fast and fresh.

makes ½ gallon

7 cups cold water, divided
¾ to 1 cup sugar (depending on desired sweetness)
1 cup fresh lime juice (see Note)
Ice, to serve

Combine 2 cups of water and the sugar in a medium-size saucepan. Bring to a boil, stirring until the sugar granules are completely dissolved. Simmer for 5 minutes. Remove the saucepan from the heat.

Add 5 cups of cold water and the lime juice. Stir to fully combine. Store in a lidded container in the refrigerator. Serve in individual glasses with ice.

Note: Before squeezing, bruise the limes on a countertop by rolling them firmly with the palm of your hand. Doing so releases the juice inside individual membranes, giving you more fresh juice upon squeezing.

Ginger Brew

makes 3 cups concentrate

----

2 cups water

1 cup pineapple juice

½ cup Turbinado sugar (see Note)

¼ pound fresh ginger, peeled and coarsely chopped

6 allspice berries

One 2-inch cinnamon stick

6 whole cloves

3 tablespoons honey

¼ cup fresh lime juice

¼ cup fresh lemon juice

Sparkling water and ice, to serve

I was first introduced to ginger brew (also sometimes confusingly referred to as ginger "beer") when I worked for a large natural foods chain in my early twenties. At the time, I had a particularly sensitive stomach. Whenever a bit of tummy distress came my way, I'd pop the tab off a glass bottle of ginger brew and slowly sip my troubles away. I've re-created the brew here. Not ginger-shy in the least, this concentrate is the very taste of the tropics.

Combine the water, pineapple juice, sugar, ginger, allspice, cinnamon, and cloves in a medium-size saucepan. Bring to a boil, cover, and simmer for 15 minutes. Remove the saucepan from the heat. Whisk in the honey, lime juice, and lemon juice. Cover and steep until cooled to room temperature. Strain the concentrate through a fine-mesh sieve placed atop a quart-size container. Compost the solids.

Transfer the strained concentrate to a lidded container, and store in the refrigerator. When ready to serve, pour about ¼ cup into a 12-ounce glass. Add ice and top off with sparkling water. Store any unused portion in the refrigerator, and use within 2 to 3 weeks.

Note: A large-granule form of sugar cane, Turbinado sugar can be found in the baking aisle of most grocery stores. If you can't source it, replace with an equal amount of light brown sugar.

Root Beer

My father is an equal opportunity root beer lover. There is no brand that he won't put to his lips. Growing up with a man so fond of the beverage, and of whom I am myself so very enamored, made me want to create my own version to proffer him during visits. If the addition of a scoop of vanilla ice cream should make its way into his glass (or yours), all the better.

makes 4 cups concentrate

4 cups water

2 tablespoons chopped fresh ginger root

1 tablespoon dried sarsaparilla root

1 tablespoon chopped dried sassafras root

½ tablespoon chopped dried licorice root

½ tablespoon dried burdock root or 2 tablespoons chopped fresh

½ tablespoon dried wintergreen leaves

4 star anise

4 cups brown sugar

Sparkling water and ice, to serve

Combine the water, ginger, sarsaparilla, sassafras, licorice, burdock, wintergreen, and star anise in a medium-size saucepan. Bring to a boil, and simmer uncovered for 15 minutes. Remove the saucepan from the heat. Whisk in the sugar until the granules fully dissolve. Cover and steep until cooled to room temperature (this may take up to 2 hours). Strain the concentrate through a fine-mesh sieve placed atop a quart-size container. Compost the solids.

Transfer the concentrate to a lidded container, and store in the refrigerator. When ready to serve, pour about 2 to 3 tablespoons into a 12-ounce glass. Add ice, top off with sparkling water, and stir gently. Use within 4 to 6 months.

Birch Beer

The licorice and wintergreen flavor associated with birch beer comes courtesy of oils derived from the sap of the birch tree itself. Similar in flavor to root beer but with slightly more mint-forward notes, birch beer is wonderfully refreshing. For an adult beverage, serve over ice with a splash of dark rum or bourbon.

Combine the water, birch bark, sassafras, lemon zest, and cloves in a medium-size saucepan. Bring to a boil, and simmer uncovered for 15 minutes. Remove the saucepan from the heat. Whisk in the sugar until the granules fully dissolve. Cover and steep until cooled to room temperature (this may take up to 2 hours). Strain the concentrate through a fine-mesh sieve placed atop a quart-size container. Compost the solids.

    Transfer the concentrate to a lidded container, and store in the refrigerator. When ready to serve, pour about 2 to 3 tablespoons into a 12-ounce glass. Add ice, top off with sparkling water, and stir gently. Use within 4 to 6 months.

makes 4 cups concentrate

4 cups water
⅔ cup birch bark
2 tablespoons chopped dried sassafras
2 tablespoons fresh lemon zest
4 whole cloves
4 cups dark brown sugar
Sparkling water and ice, to serve

GUEST RECIPE │ Cola

makes 3 cups concentrate

2 cups water

¼ teaspoon ground cinnamon

¼ teaspoon ground nutmeg

¼ teaspoon ground carda-
    mom

¼ teaspoon ground cloves

¼ teaspoon citric acid (see
    Note)

1 teaspoon minced fresh
    ginger

2 teaspoons molasses

Zest from 1 orange

Zest from 1 lemon

Zest from 1 lime

Juice from ½ lime

1-inch piece of vanilla bean,
    split open

1½ cups sugar

Seltzer, to serve

There are few things my intrepid homesteading friends Rich and Jen Or-ris aren't game to try. Backyard chickens? Kitchen garden? Mini-orchard? Homemade hot dog buns and challah? All frontiers they have conquered. The two have paired up to pen a column called Post-Consumer Pantry, *about their adventures in taking back the kitchen, that runs monthly in the western North Carolina free weekly newspaper,* Mountain Xpress. *Their cola recipe debuted in their column, but they've since tweaked it, and the result offered here rivals (and I'd argue far surpasses) that of colas famous across the globe. Bear in mind that most commercially prepared colas have caramel color added, thus darkening them. This beverage doesn't include that coloring, so it'll be considerably paler than what most of us consider the norm.*

Combine the water, cinnamon, nutmeg, cardamom, cloves, citric acid, ginger, molasses, zests, lime juice, and vanilla bean in a pot. Bring to a boil, reduce the heat to low, and simmer gently for 20 minutes. Strain the liquid through cheesecloth to catch any solids. Rinse the pot, return the liquid, and set over low heat. Add the sugar to the pot, and stir until all the sugar granules have fully dissolved.

Transfer to a lidded container, and store in the refrigerator. To serve, mix 3 tablespoons of syrup per 1 cup seltzer or to taste. Use within 2 weeks.

Note: Citric acid can be found in many natural foods stores, as well as online. It helps the soda retain its tartness and aids in preserving the soda.

Orange Soda

When I was growing up, there were very few people in my life who weren't swilling can after can of orange soda, myself included. As an adult, I've removed most sodas from my diet, especially those with any kind of food coloring. The flavor of orange soda, though, is something that's really too good to be passed on entirely. My version offers all of the refreshing flavor of orange soda, without any of the questionable ingredients.

makes 3½ cups concentrate

2 cups water

2 cups sugar

½ teaspoon citric acid (see Note)

Juice and zest from 2 oranges (strain juice; you should have roughly 1 cup juice)

Sparkling water and ice, to serve

Combine the water, sugar, citric acid, and zest in a medium-size saucepan. Bring to a boil, stirring until the sugar granules are fully dissolved. Reduce the heat to low. Simmer for 15 minutes, until the syrup has thickened. Remove the pan from the heat, cover, and allow to rest until completely cooled. Strain the syrup through a fine-mesh sieve placed atop a quart-size container. Compost the solids. Add the orange juice to the syrup. Stir to fully combine.

Transfer the concentrate to a lidded container, and store in the refrigerator. When ready to serve, pour about ¼ cup into a 12-ounce glass. Add ice, top off with sparkling water, and stir gently. Use within 1 month.

Note: Citric acid can be found in many natural foods stores, as well as online. It helps the soda retain its tartness and aids in preserving the soda.

Lemon Lime Soda

Having a good lemon lime soda recipe under your belt is a very good thing indeed. The one I'm offering here is a cinch to make, with a great tart/sweet balance and a sturdy viscosity. Serve with a scoop of homemade orange sherbert (page 77) for a sublime summertime cooler.

Combine the water, sugar, citric acid, and zests in a medium-size saucepan. Bring to a boil, stirring until the sugar granules are fully dissolved. Reduce the heat to low. Simmer for 15 minutes, until the syrup has thickened. Remove the pan from the heat, cover, and allow to rest until completely cooled.

Strain the syrup through a fine-mesh sieve placed atop a quart-size container. Compost the solids. Add the lemon and lime juices to the syrup. Stir to fully combine.

Transfer the concentrate to a lidded container, and store in the refrigerator. When ready to serve, pour about ¼ cup into a 12 ounce glass. Add ice, top off with sparkling water, and stir gently. Use within 1 month.

Note: Citric acid can be found in many natural foods stores, as well as online. It helps the soda retain its tartness and aids in preserving the soda.

makes 3½ cups concentrate

2 cups water

2 cups sugar

½ teaspoon citric acid (see Note)

Juice and zest from 2 lemons and 2 limes (strain juice; you should have roughly 1 cup juice)

Sparkling water and ice, to serve

Grapefruit Soda

2 cups water

2 cups sugar

½ teaspoon citric acid (see Note)

Juice and zest from 1 or 2 grapefruits, depending on size (strain juice; you should have roughly 1 cup juice)

Sparkling water and ice, to serve

The puckery zing of grapefruit is one of my abiding favorites. Grapefruit never fails to please, whether served in sorbet form (my Roman honeymoon sorbet of choice), rendered into marmalade, or, as here, transformed into soda. Delicious on its own, this soda would be lovely topped off with a bit of sparkling wine.

Combine the water, sugar, citric acid, and zest in a medium-size saucepan. Bring to a boil, stirring until the sugar granules are fully dissolved. Reduce the heat to low. Simmer for 15 minutes, until the syrup has thickened. Remove the pan from the heat, cover, and allow to rest until completely cooled. Strain the syrup through a fine-mesh sieve placed atop a quart-size container. Compost the solids. Add the grapefruit juice to the syrup. Stir to fully combine.

Transfer the concentrate to a lidded container, and store in the refrigerator. When ready to serve, pour about ¼ cup into a 12-ounce glass. Add ice, top off with sparkling water, and stir gently. Use within 1 month.

Note: Citric acid can be found in many natural foods stores, as well as online. It helps the soda retain its tartness and aids in preserving the soda.

Rose and Cardamom Soda

makes 2 cups concentrate

2 cups water

2 cups sugar

½ teaspoon citric acid (see Note)

6 to 8 green cardamom pods, gently cracked open

1 tablespoon rose water

Sparkling water and ice, to serve

I believe I first experienced the flavor combination of rose and cardamom in a piece of Turkish delight served, most unexpectedly, at a rural wedding in the mountains of southern Virginia. I was there helping a friend with the floral design. Relaxing with the food staff once the wedding was in full swing, I learned the parents of the bride owned the now-defunct restaurant Townhouse, and that its chefs John Shields and Karen Urie were responsible for that evening's lavish feast. The dessert table was laden with an assortment of pastries and confections without rival, and I was immeasurably inspired that evening by the flavors on offer. In this soda, rose water's floral bouquet is tempered by the resinous quality of cardamom, creating a beverage that is just as wonderful to smell as it is to sip.

Combine the water, sugar, citric acid, and cardamom pods in a medium-size saucepan. Bring to a boil, stirring until the sugar granules are fully dissolved. Reduce the heat to low. Simmer for 15 minutes, until the syrup has thickened. Remove the pan from the heat, cover, and allow to rest until completely cooled.

Strain the syrup through a fine-mesh sieve placed atop a quart-size

container. Compost the solids. Add the rose water to the syrup. Stir to fully combine.

Transfer the concentrate to a lidded container, and store in the refrigerator. When ready to serve, pour about ¼ cup into a 12-ounce glass. Add ice, top off with sparkling water, and stir gently. Use within 1 month.

Note: Citric acid can be found in many natural foods stores, as well as online. It helps the soda retain its tartness and aids in preserving the soda.

Strawberry Nectar (Spring)

makes 2 cups

2 cups hulled, chopped strawberries

1 cup apple juice

Strawberries are loaded with moisture, making them ideal candidates for a fruity beverage. When selecting specimens, look for those with the reddest flesh available. That's an indication the fruits were allowed to truly ripen before harvest, resulting in a superior flavor.

Place both ingredients in a food processor or blender. Puree until smooth. Transfer the nectar to a lidded container. Store in the refrigerator, and consume within 1 week.

FRUIT NECTARS

While I've always found fruit juices to be refreshing, I've long had a bit of an issue with the whole aspect of straining off the solids. All that fiber and other nutrients residing in the flesh should be consumed, not composted, I've steadfastly maintained. The solution, I found, lies in fruit nectars. Derived from the Greek *nektar*, or "drink of the gods," what distinguishes nectars from juices is that they contain both juice and fruit pulp. Retaining all the hydration of the juice and the nutritional benefits of the remainder of the fruit is simply the way to go.

Peach Nectar (Summer)

Should you happen to find yourself with a bumper crop of peaches, here's what I suggest. First, eat as many fresh, ripe specimens as your stomach will allow. Second, make numerous batches of peach pies, crisps, and cobblers. Follow that up with peach jam, and, finally, puree up a pitcher or two of peach nectar. You'll then have enjoyed the glorious fruits of summer in their various incarnations and end on a sweet, creamy, smooth note.

Using a small paring knife, make a small *X* on the bottom of each peach. Fill a large bowl with ice and cold water, creating an ice bath. Set aside. Fill a medium-size saucepan or small stock pot with water; bring to a boil. Drop in all of the peaches at once. Boil 1 minute, remove with a slotted spoon, and place immediately into the ice bath. The skins should now slide off easily. Once the skins are removed, pit the peaches, and coarsely chop the flesh.

Place the chopped peaches, water, and lemon juice in a food processor or blender. Puree until smooth. If desired, adjust the sweetness of the nectar by adding either apple or white grape juice, to taste. Transfer the nectar to a lidded container. Store in the refrigerator, and consume within 1 week.

makes 4 to 5 cups

Ice and cold water, for peeling peaches

1½ pounds ripe peaches

2 cups water

1 tablespoon lemon juice

Apple or white grape juice, to taste (optional)

Pear Nectar (Autumn)

makes 4 to 5 cups

2 pounds ripe pears, peeled,
    cored, and chopped
3 cups water
1 tablespoon lemon juice
½ cup apple juice (optional)

For me, the stretch of days from late September to late December simply isn't itself without the appearance of a bit of pear nectar. Served alongside hot coffee and a stack of apple pancakes, or enjoyed spiked with bourbon around an outdoor fire, pear nectar brings the essence of autumn to life.

Place the pears and water into a medium-size saucepan. Bring the water to a boil and cook over medium-high heat for 5 to 7 minutes. Remove the pan from the heat, and allow to cool 15 to 20 minutes.

Puree in a food processor or blender with the lemon juice until smooth. If desired, adjust the sweetness of the nectar by adding the apple juice. Transfer the nectar to a lidded container. Store in the refrigerator, and consume within 1 week.

Citrus Nectar (Winter)

makes 4 to 5 cups

2 pounds winter citrus of your
    choice (use a combination
    of blood oranges, clemen-
    tines, satsumas, pomelos,
    grapefruit, and other
    seasonal citrus fruits)
2 cups water
1 tablespoon lemon juice

My husband's parents live in Sarasota, Florida. Accordingly, they are surrounded by countless citrus orchards. Come wintertime, when the landscape around our mountain home is barren and bleak, they're enveloped by the sights, scents, and flavors of oranges, grapefruit, tangerines, clementines, and other citrus coming to their peak of ripeness. Fortunately for us, they always ship a box of their area's finest up our way. That box of sunshine brightens our dark mornings for weeks. Pureeing a bit of it into a citrus nectar is another way to keep the party going.

Peel and seed the citrus. Break the fruit into individual segments. Place the segmented fruit, water, and lemon juice in a food processor or blender. Puree until smooth. Transfer the nectar to a lidded container. Store in the refrigerator, and consume within 1 week.

Quenched: Pear Nectar

The summer following my freshman year of college, in 1995, it quickly became obvious to me that I'd need to get a job. Though I'd worked all school year long in the library, the job was part of my work-trade payment arrangement and didn't provide any pocket change. Music, movies, food, and new clothes—all essential items for a nineteen-year-old—needed to be purchased, enjoyed, consumed, and showcased (although my penchant those days for garments was more of the Salvation Army ilk than the Sears and Roebuck variety).

I was living in Asheville, North Carolina, and a new bakery had recently opened. Modeled after the Parisian bakeries of which the owners were so enamored, Blue Moon Bakery became my place of employment, as it also was for my brother and my boyfriend. Known for their overstuffed sandwiches (the roast beef and Brie got me superexcited) and tasty side dishes during lunchtime, it was their breads and pastries that brought on the crowds each weekend. Friday's challah was golden and eggy and gorgeously braided, and coveted by households across town. Saturday's parade of pastries had crowds lining up outside the door as the first rays of morning sunlight flooded the bakery. Pain au chocolat, apricot turnovers, buttery croissants the likes of which I had never tasted were scooped up, packaged in sturdy white boxes, and sent out the door, emptying the pastry case before noon.

It was during my tenure at Blue Moon Bakery that I first encountered pear nectar. A cold drink case was regularly stocked with beverages I'd never heard of. Alongside Perrier (the southern towns I'd grown up in carried no such fancy French bubble water) and San Pellegrino limonata were bottles of Looza pear nectar. On my lunch break, I'd happily twist the cap off the bottle and quench my thirst with its fruity, creamy deliciousness, reveling in its ambrosial nectar. I might have been in a western North Carolina mountain town, but I might as well have been in a Parisian café.

To this day, pear nectar always takes me back to the exciting days of my late teens. College, my first serious boyfriend, discovering my interests and sense of self, taking a class on existentialism (holy *Being and Nothingness*!)—those tumultuous days set the tone for the woman I have grown to become.

Ginger Shrub

makes 2 cups concentrate

----

1 cup peeled, chopped fresh ginger

1½ cups apple cider vinegar

¾ cup sugar

Water, still or sparkling, to serve

Our good friends Jen and Jon are both private school teachers in Atlanta. They come to visit frequently and typically bring some kind of delectable food item scored in the big city with them. One recent offering was an amber-colored bottle of ginger shrub. A vinegar-based beverage, shrubs can be rendered out of countless fruits, herbs, and spices. Several tablespoons are topped off with still or sparkling water. The resulting beverage is powerfully invigorating and deeply satisfying.

Combine the ginger and apple cider vinegar in a small saucepan. Bring just to the boiling point. Remove the pan from the heat, and allow to cool 15 to 20 minutes. Transfer the contents to a heatproof container (such as a Mason jar), cover with a lid, and steep at room temperature for 48 hours. Give the jar a few shakes each day as it infuses. Strain the infusion through a fine-mesh sieve over a small saucepan. Compost the solids.

Add the sugar to the ginger infusion. Bring to a boil, stirring until all of the sugar granules are dissolved. Reduce the heat to low, and simmer for 5 minutes. Remove from the heat, allow to cool in the saucepan for about 15 minutes, then transfer to a lidded container. Label and store in the refrigerator. Consume within 6 months.

To serve, place 1 to 2 tablespoons in an 8- to 10-ounce glass. Dilute with water (either still or sparkling), iced tea, sparkling fruit juice, lemonade, or other beverage of your choice for a puckery drink.

GUEST RECIPE | Blood Orange Shrub

Marisa McClellan knows her way around a kitchen. The force behind both the book and the blog Food in Jars, *this Philadelphia resident produces all manner of pickles, chutneys, jams, syrups, jellies, granola, and so very much more from her urban kitchen. Here she's graciously sharing her recipe for blood orange shrub. Capitalizing on the ruby-tinged juice that makes a brief cameo each winter, Marisa likes a bit of sour with her sweet. The resulting concentrate is laced with gorgeous color and full of tangy perfection.*

Combine the blood orange juice and sugar in a glass or ceramic bowl or jar. Allow the mixture to sit until the sugar is entirely dissolved. This should take about 1 hour (giving it a quick stir every time you walk by will help things along). Once there are no visible signs of granulated sugar in the juice, add the vinegar and stir until everything is fully combined. Label and store in a lidded container in the refrigerator. Consume within 6 months.

To serve, place 1 to 2 tablespoons in an 8- to 10-ounce glass. Dilute with water (either still or sparkling), iced tea, sparkling fruit juice, lemonade, or other beverage of your choice for a puckery drink. For the daring, add a splash of gin!

makes 2½ cups concentrate

1 cup blood orange juice (from about 4 to 6 blood oranges)
1 cup sugar
¾ cup apple cider vinegar
Water, still or sparkling, to serve

Kombucha

makes ½ gallon

3 quarts filtered water

1 cup organic white sugar

4 organic black tea bags

½ cup starter liquid (this will come with the kombucha culture)

1 kombucha culture (see Note)

Composed of water, black tea, sugar, and a mother culture, this tonic beverage can be made at home for considerably less cost than incurred by purchasing it premade. Kombucha is rife with enzymes, probiotics, amino acids, antioxidants, and a host of other beneficial nutrients. It's been consumed around the world for centuries, making its way west in the past few decades and into the larger cultural landscape over the last few years. Admittedly, kombucha's sensory properties make it the sort of beverage only a "mother" could love. The taste is reminiscent of old beer and vinegar, and the culture looks like a slab of human skin suspended in a murky solution—overcoming the olfactory and visual impact of kombucha is a bit daunting in the beginning. It's sour and puckery and fizzy all at once.

Bring 3 quarts of water to a low boil in a medium-size saucepan. Add the sugar, and stir until completely dissolved. Remove the pan from the heat, add tea bags, and steep for 15 minutes. Remove the tea bags, and allow the tea to cool to room temperature.

Pour the tea into a large, sterilized glass container (I use a square glass canister with a lid, found at a home goods store). Add the starter liquid and stir with a metal spoon. Place the culture on top of the tea, with the more shiny side facing upward. Lay a kitchen cloth or cloth napkin over the top and secure it firmly with a rubber band or piece of string. Transfer the container to a dark, room-temperature area (I use my pantry). Allow to culture for 2 to 3 weeks, depending on how intense of a flavor you desire. Keep in mind that a longer culturing time results in a more sour, carbonated kombucha (my preference!).

When you feel it's the flavor you want, transfer most of the kombucha to a lidded container and store in the refrigerator. Keep the mother in the culturing container, along with at least ½ cup liquid. Begin another batch of tea, cool, and add to the culturing container. Continue doing this for a constant supply of kombucha.

Over time, your mother culture will begin producing "babies," visible secondary layers. Remove those layers and give them to friends.

Otherwise, you'll need to add them to the compost pile in order for the mother to remain strong and viable.

To serve, either take straight shots or dilute with juice or water (still or sparkling). I love to drink my kombucha by pouring about ¼ cup into a 12-ounce glass, adding ¼ cup unsweetened cranberry juice, and topping it off with sparkling water.

Note: The kombucha culture can be purchased online or sourced from a nearby friend who brews kombucha him- or herself; the latter is how I obtained mine. If you are fortunate enough to source a SCOBY (a symbiotic colony of bacterial yeasts, or the kombucha culture) and starter liquid from a nearby friend, you'll need a sterilized glass jar with a lid for transporting it home. Don't use plastic, as food debris or flavors trapped inside the plastic can compromise your culture and starter liquid.

Quenched: Kombucha

There are some homes you visit that leave an indelible etch on your mind's eye. My mom, a huge fan of any Parade of Homes tour, took us into countless spec houses during my childhood. One of them, which I'll never forget, greeted visitors with a circular fish tank built right into the wall of the foyer. Later, in my teens, I lived for seven months in a converted tobacco barn in the tiny western North Carolina mountain town of Montreat. Covered by lofty tulip poplars and oaks, the house was set in a creekside ravine and had a giant stone hearth in the living room, French doors leading onto porches in two of the bedrooms, and an ever-present scent of wood smoke and ageing wood. It was glorious.

Then there's Beth and Christopher's house. Maintaining a farm and a flourishing nonprofit consulting practice, Beth and Christopher live and work in the Swannanoa Valley located just east of Asheville, North Carolina. Several years ago, I ventured to tour their farm, pepper them with natural growing questions, and pick up a SCOBY—the symbiotic colony of bacterial yeasts that's needed if you want to brew a batch of kombucha. You can purchase them online, but I loved the idea of using one that was already thriving on the wild yeasts present in my own stomping grounds. I put out a solicitation online, and Beth answered my query.

While acquiring the SCOBY was all well and good, it was the tour of their grounds and house that stood out to me the most that day. They had a small pond with a flock of ducks, several beehives, a flock of laying hens, fruit trees, a permaculture-designed garden, greenhouses, and a yurt that housed them while their home was under construction and would later keep guests and farm interns comfortable. Their house, in its former incarnation, had been a horse barn. It was modest but solidly built, employing a number of energy-efficient and green-building practices in its construction. It was warm and inviting and approachable. I remember thinking that the house reflected its owners, as the adjectives describing it could just as easily be applied to Beth and Christopher. I might have physically left with a SCOBY that day, one that would go on to quench my thirst for many mornings to come; however, mentally, I took away a great deal more. From gardening techniques to homes that speak to the character of their residents, that visit was one I'll not soon forget.

Agua de Jamaica

makes ½ gallon

- - - - - - - - - - - - - - - - - -

8 cups water, divided

⅔ cup dried hibiscus flowers

½ cup granulated sugar

2 tablespoons dried orange peel

1 cinnamon stick, broken into
      pieces

½ tablespoon dried chopped
      lemongrass

½ tablespoon allspice berries

½ teaspoon whole cloves

Juice from 1 lime

Ice, to serve

- - - - - - - - - - - - - - - - - -

My friend Eli runs a mobile coffee cart called Ursa Minor. While winter-time purchases are typically composed of hot lattes and double espressos, come summer, the offerings turn considerably icier. One of his hot weather treats is Agua de Jamaica. The hibiscus flower is the true star here, sidling up next to island spices like cinnamon, allspice, and cloves to create a tea that's equal parts floral, spicy, and sweet. Here's my attempt at re-creating his stellar summertime soother.

Place 4 cups of water, hibiscus flowers, sugar, orange peel, cinnamon stick, lemongrass, allspice, and cloves into a medium-size stainless-steel pot. Stir gently to combine the ingredients. Bring to a boil over medium-high heat. Reduce the heat to low and simmer for 15 minutes, until the sugar is fully dissolved. Remove the pot from the heat, cover with a lid, and steep for 1 hour. Strain the liquid through a fine-mesh sieve set over a pitcher. Compost the solids.

Add the remaining 4 cups of water and the lime juice to the pitcher. Stir to fully combine. Cover the pitcher with a lid, and store in the refrigerator. Serve the Agua de Jamaica well chilled in individual glasses over ice. Consume within 1 week.

Watermelon Agua Fresca

Certain clichés exist for a reason. For me, hearing about the degree to which pregnant women crave watermelon proved undeniably true during my own tenure. I could've eaten my weight in the juicy fruit. Alongside eating it whole or tossed into fruit salads, I also consumed it in liquid form. Pregnant or not, this deeply thirst-quenching beverage is what you want to be sipping when the sun is high, bright, and scorching.

Puree the watermelon and water in a food processor or blender until smooth. Depending on the capacity of your machine, you may need to do this in two batches. Strain the puree through a fine-mesh sieve placed over a pitcher. Compost the solids. Add the lime juice and honey to the watermelon juice. Whisk to fully combine.

Cover the pitcher with a lid, and store in the refrigerator. Serve in individual glasses with ice. Consume within 1 week.

makes ½ gallon

4 pounds watermelon, seeded and cut into chunks

1½ cups cold water

2 tablespoons lime juice

1 tablespoon honey

Ice, to serve

Water Infusions

Flavor additions (choose one):

   2 cups fresh herbs or flowers
      for an herbal or floral
      infusion
   ¼ cup spices for a spice
      infusion
   1 cup fruits or vegetables for a
      fruit or vegetable infusion

8 cups water

I like routine. Every morning, as soon as I step into the kitchen, I give the cats their morning food, let the dogs outside to attend to their bladders, and then pour myself a big glass of water. I then continue to consume water all day long, typically, though, gussying it up a bit first. Infusing water with fresh herbs, spices, and produce is a fantastic way of injecting a bit of interest into your water. It's phenomenally easy to do and considerably less costly than purchasing premade versions. This recipe is easily doubled.

Place the infusing agent(s) of your choosing in a container. Top off with water, cover with a secure lid, and give the contents a good shake. Either leave in full sun for 5 to 8 hours, depending on how intense of a flavor you wish to achieve or leave to infuse in the refrigerator. A glass container is ideal for doing a sun infusion, as the sun's rays can best penetrate and warm such a vessel. Store in the refrigerator, and use within 2 to 3 days.

INFUSION INGREDIENTS

The following details a number of edible flowers, herbs, spices, and fruits and vegetables that would be perfect candidates for infusions. The amounts of infusing ingredients I listed are for only one ingredient at a time. That said, if you want to infuse things together, that's fine as well. Be sure to avoid use of any plant matter that has been sprayed with a pesticide or herbicide; also, avoid consuming any matter found growing alongside busy roadways, as such plants will have accumulated a number of noxious substances in their roots and tissues.

· *Herbal Infusions:* Anise hyssop, apple mint, basil, calendula, chamomile, chives, dill, lemon balm, lemongrass, lemon verbena, marjoram, mint, oregano, parsley, peppermint, rosemary, sage (pineapple sage makes a wonderful herbal infusion), spearmint, and thyme (especially lemon thyme).

- *Floral Infusions:* Bee balm, borage, carnations, dianthus, fennel fronds, hibiscus, hollyhock, honeysuckle flowers (avoid the poisonous berries), jasmine flowers, Johnny-jump-ups, lavender buds, lilac, nasturtiums, pansies, roses, scented geraniums, sunflowers, and violets.
- *Spice Infusions:* Allspice berries, cardamom pods, whole cloves, crystallized ginger pieces, fennel seeds, juniper berries, star anise, and vanilla bean.
- *Fruit and Vegetable Infusions:* Citrus peel (lemons, limes, grapefruits, oranges, tangerines, tangelos, etc.), cranberries, cucumber slices, fresh berries, fresh ginger slices, and melon cubes.

invigorating

Sometimes what you need is a little kick. A jolt. A jumpstart. The coffees and teas found here were created with that very thing in mind. Once you begin creating beverages previously enjoyed at the coffee shop in the comfort of your own home, you'll be thrilled by both all the money you'll save and all the flavor you'll gain.

Iced Coffee

makes 2½ cups
concentrate

2⅔ cups coarsely ground
    coffee

4 cups water

Ice plus water, milk, or
    half-and-half, to serve
    (optional)

----

*Each time my husband downs an iced coffee, he consumes it as though it
will be his very last beverage while living. In under two minutes, his cup is
drained of its contents and he's already clamoring for more. To give him his
fix while not spending our mortgage on purchased coffees, I sought out the
best means of creating iced coffee at home. An article in* Imbibe *magazine
served as the inspiration for this recipe. Depending on the frequency with
which your household consumes iced coffee, double, triple, or, dare I say,
quadruple the measurements accordingly.*

Combine the coffee and water in whatever container you'll be brewing
in. You can use a jar, bowl, or vessel with a built-in filter, such as a French
press or similar item for brewing. Stir with a spoon until all of the coffee
grinds have been saturated with water. Cover the container with a lid,
and leave to infuse at room temperature for 12 to 24 hours. The longer it
steeps, the stronger the flavor.

   Filter the coffee. If you've infused it in a bowl or jar, strain the concentrate through a fine-mesh sieve, metal coffee filter, or fine cheesecloth placed atop a bowl. If you've infused it in a vessel with a built-in
filter, deploy the plunger to press the grounds down or follow the manufacturer's instructions for filtering.

   Place the concentrate in a container, cover with a lid, and store in
the refrigerator. To serve, dilute with water, milk, or half-and-half and
ice. The amount of liquid needed for dilution is at your discretion. Use
within 1 week.

Flavored Coffees

makes 8 cups

Coffee beans (enough for an
    8-cup pot of coffee)
Flavoring of your choice
    (choose one):

Seeds from 4 green carda-
    mom pods (see Note)
2 whole cloves
One 11-inch piece cinna-
    mon stick or 1 teaspoon
    ground cinnamon
½ star anise
1 teaspoon freshly grated
    nutmeg
Seeds from 1-inch piece of
    vanilla bean (see Note)

In college a former boyfriend and I frequently tried our hand at passing as adults by purchasing flavored coffees. At the time (for me, at least), brewing up pots of coffee redolent of nuts and spices was the pinnacle of adulthood—and so very chic. As I grew older and truly entered adulthood, I got wise to many of the artificial ingredients used to create "Hazelnut Bliss" and "Pumpkin Patch." Not wanting to completely give up on the pleasures of flavored coffee, I set out to create my own. It turns out that doing so couldn't be easier. Begin with the freshest coffee beans and spices you can find. Whether you're eighteen or eighty, these coffees have wise adult *written all over them.*

Place enough coffee beans for an 8-cup pot of coffee and the spice of your choosing into a coffee grinder. Grind to your desired texture. Brew coffee using a French press, Moka pot, or drip coffee maker according to the manufacturer's instructions.

If not using the ground blend right away, store it in a metal canister, glass jar, or brown coffee bag. While best if used upon grinding, the blend will stay fresh for up to 1 week at room temperature or 3 to 4 weeks in the freezer.

Note: To remove the seeds from cardamom pods, hit the pod with the back of a spoon. Once cracked open you can easily extract the small black seeds.

To remove the seeds from a vanilla bean pod, using a fine-tipped knife, slice the pod open lengthwise, then scrape out the tiny seed flecks with the knife tip.

Traditional Iced Tea

To grow up in the southeastern United States is to know iced tea quite well. Sweet and unsweetened versions are available at all restaurants, both fine and fast. Both my mother and my grandmother have kept gallon pitchers of iced tea in their refrigerators whether snow or sunshine blankets the ground outdoors. Here is my family's recipe for creating the perfect pitcher.

Place the tea bags in a ceramic bowl, pitcher, or heatproof glass container. Pour the boiling water over the tea bags. Steep for 4 minutes. Add 4 cups cold water. Remove the tea bags taking care not to squeeze them.

Store in a lidded container in the refrigerator. Serve cold with ice and, if desired, lemon wedges and simple syrup. Use within 1 week.

Note: I like to use Ceylon tea when making iced tea, but Earl Grey makes for a lovely, citrus-imbued iced tea, as well.

makes ½ gallon

6 black tea bags (see Note)
4 cups boiling water
4 cups cold water
Ice, to serve
Lemon wedges and simple
    syrup, to serve (optional;
    recipe follows)

For the *Simple Syrup*

1 cup water
2 cups sugar or 1½ cups
    honey or agave nectar

Mint Iced Tea

makes ½ gallon

6 black tea bags

4 cups boiling water

4 cups cold water

8 large stems of fresh mint

2 ripe peaches, thinly sliced
   (optional)

Ice, to serve

On a hot summer day, few things expediently cool the way that mint does. Whether you're enjoying it hard in a mojito or soft in a bit of iced tea, a little bit of mint goes a very long way. I've partnered it here with black tea, creating a tea that perks you up while cooling you off. For a summery variation, this tea is also delicious with the addition of fresh, ripe peaches. Thinly slice two peaches and add to the infusion after straining off the mint.

Place the tea bags in a ceramic bowl or pitcher or a heatproof glass container. Pour the boiling water over the tea bags. Steep for 4 minutes. Remove the tea bags taking care not to squeeze them. Add fresh mint and 4 cups cold water. Cover and steep for 30 minutes. Remove the mint leaves. Compost the solids.

Transfer the tea to a lidded container, add the peaches if desired, and store in the refrigerator. Serve cold, with ice. Use within 1 week.

Lemongrass and Ginger Iced Tea

makes ½ gallon

----

2 lemongrass stalks

3 tablespoons minced fresh
    ginger (from one knob
    peeled ginger)

8 cups water, divided

¼ cup honey

3 black tea bags

Ice, to serve

I came a bit late to lemongrass. Growing up in the southeastern United States in the 1980s, it just wasn't really part of the culinary lexicon. Nowadays, it's easy to source a stalk or two at area grocery stores and foreign foods stores. Married to a healthy bit of ginger, some black tea, and a generous lashing of honey, this iced tea is aromatic, fragrant, zesty, and cooling, all at once—all good things.

Prepare the lemongrass by cutting off the green stalks and the root bottom of the lemongrass and removing the tough outer leaves. Pound the lemongrass stalks with the flat side of a knife to release their juices. Slice thinly.

Place the sliced lemongrass, ginger, and 4 cups of water into a medium-size saucepan. Bring to a boil. Reduce the heat to low, and simmer for 10 minutes. Remove the saucepan from the heat. Add the honey, and whisk to fully combine. Cover with a lid, and steep for 15 minutes. Strain the syrup through a fine-mesh sieve placed atop a pitcher. Compost the solids.

Bring the remaining 4 cups of water to a boil. Place the tea bags in a bowl, and pour the boiling water over them. Steep for 4 minutes. Remove the tea bags taking care not to squeeze them. Add the tea to the syrup in the pitcher. Stir to combine.

Cover with a lid, and store in the refrigerator. Serve cold, with ice. Use within 1 week.

Wild Zinger Tea

makes ½ gallon

8 cups water

2 tablespoons dried chopped
lemongrass (or 1 table-
spoon fresh)

1 tablespoon dried rose hips

1 tablespoon dried spearmint

1 tablespoon dried hibiscus
leaves

1 tablespoon dried orange peel

1 teaspoon dried rose petals

1 teaspoon dried ginger root

1 teaspoon dried licorice root

The cheerful decorative boxes characteristic of Celestial Seasonings teas have long been a household staple for me. Their Red Zinger is almost always found in my pantry, until recently, that is. Always wanting to try my hand at DIY versions of prepared food items, I set out to create a custom version. My goal was to create the best of their tea while combining it with ingredients used in another beloved tisane, the Wild Orange made by Tazo. The ingredients used here can all be readily found in natural foods stores, as well as online.

Bring the water to a boil. Place all of the remaining ingredients in a tea pot. Pour the boiling water over them, cover with a lid, and steep for 15 minutes. Strain the tea through a fine-mesh sieve placed atop a pitcher. Compost the solids.

Cover the tea with a lid, and store in the refrigerator. Serve cold. Use within 1 week.

Thai Iced Tea

One of the best parts of having friends living in San Francisco is going out to visit them. The culinary offerings available in the city by the bay are sensational. I'm especially fond of the countless Thai restaurants the city boasts, and I make a point of gorging myself on Pad See Ew and green papaya salad whenever I'm out there. I also make sure to enjoy an icy glass of Thai iced tea during my forays. Since I don't make it to San Francisco as much as I or my friend would like, I try to bring bits of the city's eats home, as is the case with this Thai Iced Tea. Sweet, creamy, and spicy, the tea hits every flavor note. If you can find orange blossom water, it really does take the tea from super to sublime.

Bring the water to a boil in a medium-size saucepan. Add the tea, vanilla bean, star anise, cinnamon, cardamom, cloves, and tamarind paste, if using. Reduce the heat to low, and simmer for 5 minutes. Strain the tea through a fine-mesh sieve set atop a mixing bowl. Compost the solids. Add the sugar, sweetened condensed milk, and orange blossom water, if using, to the tea. Whisk until the sugar granules have completely dissolved.

Transfer the tea to a lidded container. Store in the refrigerator. To serve, place several ice cubes into a 10- to 12-ounce glass. Pour 1 cup of tea into the glass, top with 2 tablespoons evaporated milk, and stir with a spoon to combine. Use tea within 1 week.

makes 4 cups

3 cups water

¼ cup + 2 tablespoons loose
    Ceylon tea

½ vanilla bean

2 star anise

Two 2-inch cinnamon sticks

4 green cardamom pods

1 teaspoon whole cloves

½ teaspoon tamarind paste
    (optional)

3 tablespoons sugar

3 tablespoons sweetened
    condensed milk

Splash of orange blossom
    water (optional)

Ice and ½ cup evaporated
    milk, divided, to serve

satisfying and indulgent

There are days when my taste buds want something creamy and rich and abundantly flavorful. These are the beverages for those days. Milks and shakes and other chilly delights pack a powerful punch, filling the belly while cooling the body and, oftentimes, calming the mind. Added to your breakfast cereal or in your morning cuppa, sipped through paper straws or curlicued ones, these drinks deliver just what you need, right when you need it.

Almond Milk

makes 4 cups

1 cup almonds (raw, unsalted)
4 cups boiling water

The key to creating wonderful almond milk at home, I've discovered, is heating up the almonds. And by heating, I mean scalding the mess out of them. Following up on a tip found online, it turns out that just pureeing almonds with water doesn't provide nearly the same degree of creaminess as is gained by first scalding them and then allowing the mixture to steep. If you prefer a sweetened or flavored almond milk, simply add dates, vanilla, or spices to the liquid when pureeing.

Combine the almonds and boiling water in a heatproof glass or ceramic bowl. Let rest for 5 minutes. Transfer the mixture to a food processor or blender. Puree for 2 minutes, until smooth. Strain the liquid through a sieve set atop a bowl, pressing on the pureed nuts with a metal spoon to extract as much liquid as possible. Compost the solids or set them aside for another use.

Transfer the almond milk to a lidded container. Store in the refrigerator. Use within 5 to 7 days.

Rice Milk

makes 4 cups

1 cup long-grain brown rice
4 cups water

When I learned just how easy it was to make rice milk at home, I was equal parts enthralled and appalled. While ecstatic to learn of its ease, I was a bit aghast at how much I'd spent on packaged rice milk over the years. Well, no more! Homemade rice milk, in my estimation, is also considerably more flavorful, as doing it yourself allows you to select the freshest rice available to you. For a chocolate version, simply add a few tablespoons of cocoa powder when pureeing.

Place the rice and water into a food processor or blender. Pulse until the rice grains have broken down a bit. Transfer the mixture to a glass or ceramic bowl. Cover with a plate or lid, and leave at room temperature for 4 hours. Return the mixture to the food processor or blender. Puree until smooth. Strain the mixture through a fine-mesh sieve or fine cheesecloth set over a bowl. Compost the solids.

Transfer the rice milk to a lidded container. Store in the refrigerator. Use within 5 to 7 days.

QUENCHED: RICE MILK

From 1996 to about two days before New Year's Eve 1999, I lived in Washington, D.C. It was during those four years that I adopted a vegan diet. Nuts, legumes, fruits, and vegetables were my foods of choice, and my passion. I began amassing a small library of vegan and vegetarian cookbooks, spending hours dog-earing recipes I'd like to try, and writing up shopping lists of ingredients to procure.

To place myself in a sort of ground zero for my newfound interest (and get an employee discount on all the tofu and soy yogurt I was purchasing), I began working at natural foods stores in the area. From Whole Foods in Arlington to the Good Food Store and Yes! Natural Gourmet in Adams Morgan, I entrenched myself in the land of quinoa, almond butter, and kale chips. It was during these early days of my natural foods infatuation that I discovered rice milk.

Packaged in Tetra Pak aseptic boxes, rice milk came in a variety of flavors, and I made good use of my discount purchasing power to sample the range. Original, vanilla, chocolate—I tasted them all. Soon, my morning granola was given a hearty douse, I substituted it for cow's milk in baked goods recipes, and later, I discovered delicious frozen novelties involving oatmeal sandwich cookies cradling a minty version, covered in melted carob.

I no longer maintain a vegan diet, having reentered the world of dairy products over a decade ago. I'm thankful for that time, though, and for the world of foods and cultures it introduced me to. The Whole Foods in Arlington employed a number of Ethiopians while Yes! Natural Gourmet introduced me to South Korean owners and staff from Nicaragua, El Salvador, Guyana, and Ivory Coast. I sampled foods from their home countries during lunch breaks and had a regular French lesson each Tuesday with Diego, who left Ivory Coast to work as a high school instructor in Paris. I quenched my thirst while gaining a world of knowledge.

Coconut Milk

*If you've got some unsweetened coconut on hand, you're already halfway to-
ward creating homemade coconut milk. With a bit of water and a modest
amount of effort, the stuff that makes curries lovely and piña coladas shine
can be yours. Do double duty and fashion macaroons out of the leftover
coconut meat.*

makes 4 cups

4 cups boiling water
2 cups unsweetened shredded
    coconut

Combine the boiling water and coconut in a food processor or blender.
Puree until creamy. Strain the liquid through a fine-mesh sieve lined
with cheesecloth and set atop a bowl, pressing on the pureed coconut
with a metal spoon to extract as much liquid as possible. Compost the
solids or set them aside for another use. Repeat this process until the
milky liquid contains no solids.

Transfer the coconut milk to a lidded container, and store in the refrigerator. Use within 1 week.

Buttermilk

makes 4 cups

4 cups whole milk
⅔ cup buttermilk with live,
active cultures (check
label) or 1 packet of dried
buttermilk culture

I have known the pleasures of buttermilk for as long as I can recall. My maternal grandmother is deeply fond of the puckery beverage and, despite repeated replies of "No, I'm sorry, we don't have any," continues to request a glass of it whenever dining out. I share her love of buttermilk and try to always have some on hand. It does wonders to fried chicken if first brined in it (add some smoky paprika for extra flavor) and takes biscuits to a whole other level. It also makes a fine ice cream, especially if served alongside fresh peaches or nectarines.

With the help of a dairy or instant-read thermometer, warm the milk over medium-high heat until it reaches 85°F. Transfer the warm milk to a glass or ceramic bowl. Whisk in the buttermilk or dried culture until fully combined. Place a metal lid or ceramic plate over the bowl. Leave to culture at room temperature for 12 hours.

Transfer the cultured buttermilk to a lidded container, and store in the refrigerator. Use within 1 to 2 weeks.

Kefir

A fermented milk beverage, kefir is believed to have originated in the Caucasus mountains. It is similar in many ways to yogurt, only thinner. The hardest part of making kefir, I've found, lies simply in obtaining live kefir grains, which are typically not available between the boxes of butter and cubes of packaged cheese at grocery stores. They are available, though, at a number of natural foods stores, as well as online.

makes 4 cups

4 cups whole, skim, or low-fat
    milk (cow or goat)
¼ cup live kefir grains

Place the milk and kefir grains in a glass or ceramic container (I like to use a quart-size Mason jar). Stir gently with a metal spoon. Lay a lightweight kitchen cloth across the top of the container. Leave to culture at room temperature for 24 hours. At the end of culturing time, give the liquid a gentle stir with a metal spoon. Strain the liquid through a fine-mesh sieve placed atop a bowl. Take care to not press on the kefir grains while straining. Set aside the solids.

Transfer the strained liquid to a lidded container, and store in the refrigerator. Use within 3 weeks. Place the moist kefir grains in a separate lidded container. Store in the refrigerator until ready to make a fresh batch. The grains will last indefinitely if well cared for.

Horchata

makes 4 cups

1 cup long-grain brown rice
4 cups water
1 cinnamon stick, broken into
    pieces
½ cup granulated sugar
2 teaspoons ground cinnamon
Ice, to serve

My very first date with my husband took place January 1, 2007, at a Salvadoran restaurant in Asheville, North Carolina. Among their numerous delicious menu options, Tomato Cocina Latina offered a delicious horchata. I'd never had the rice-based beverage before meeting Glenn and will forever associate its flavor with our early courtship. The rice in the recipe needs to infuse for four hours, so plan ahead when making this horchata.

Place the rice, water, and cinnamon stick into a food processor or blender. Pulse until the rice grains have broken down a bit. Transfer the mixture to a glass or ceramic bowl. Cover with a plate or lid, and leave at room temperature for 4 hours. Return the mixture to the food processor or blender. Puree until smooth. Strain the mixture through a fine-mesh sieve or fine cheesecloth set over a bowl. Compost the solids.

Transfer the strained-off liquid to a pitcher. Add the sugar and ground cinnamon; whisk until fully combined. Refrigerate the horchata until well chilled. Serve in individual glasses over ice. Use within 2 to 3 days.

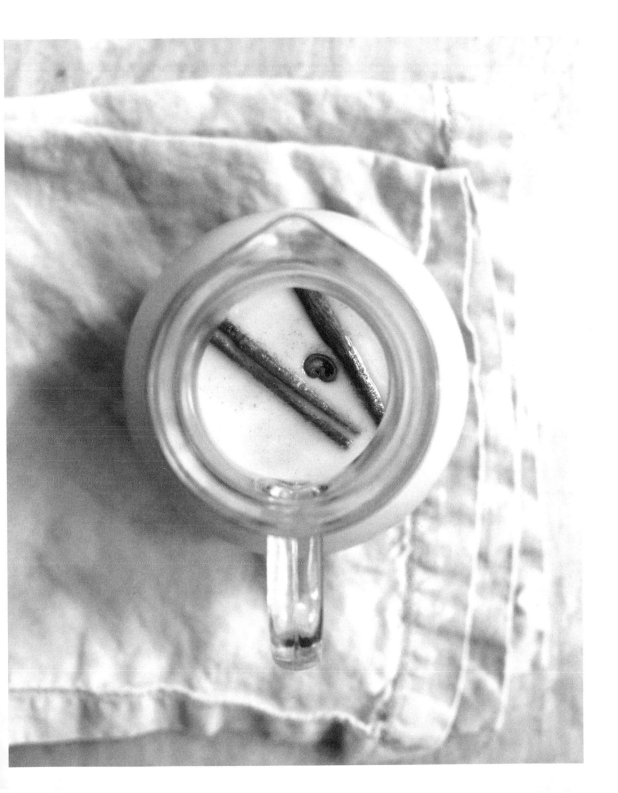

Mango Lassi

The key to creating a mango lassi of untold deliciousness, I've found, is beginning with ripe mangoes. If your mango has no "give" when gently pressed, move on to the next one. If, however, it is super squishy when handled, it might have turned. Be very Goldilocks in your mango selecting and seek out specimens that aren't too firm and aren't too soft. The result is completely worth the fussiness.

Place yogurt, mango, water, honey, and cardamom, and rose water if using, in a food processor or blender. Puree until smooth.

Transfer the puree to a lidded container, and store in the refrigerator. Use within 1 to 2 days. Serve over ice in 8- to 10-ounce glasses.

makes 4 cups

2 cups whole milk yogurt
1 cup mango chunks (from approximately 2 ripe mangoes)
½ cup water
1 to 2 tablespoons honey (amount needed will depend on the ripeness of the mangoes used)
½ teaspoon ground cardamom (optional)
1 teaspoon rose water (optional)
Ice, to serve

Perfect Vanilla Milkshake

makes 2 servings

2 cups vanilla ice cream
½ cup whole milk
2 teaspoons vanilla extract

An ideal milkshake is all about the straw. When placed in a milkshake that's fashioned too thick, a straw not only will remain fully upright but also won't draw up any shake when sucked on. Too thin and the straw is all loosey-goosey and the liquid excessively runny. The perfect milkshake holds a straw just off-kilter, in the fashion of the Leaning Tower of Pisa, and produces a shake both yielding and substantial. What I'm offering you here is my dairy version of the iconic Italian landmark. If you'd like to gild the lily, several flavoring options are listed.

Put two 10-ounce glasses in the freezer. Place all of the ingredients in a blender or food processor. Puree until creamy and smooth. Transfer the mixture to the chilled glasses. Serve immediately with straws or long-handled spoons.

FLAVORFUL VANILLA SHAKE ADDITIONS

· 2 tablespoons whiskey and 1 teaspoon orange zest
· 1 teaspoon ground cardamom and 1 teaspoon rose water
· ½ cup fresh peach slices and 1 teaspoon freshly grated nutmeg

Perfect Chocolate Milkshake

I can't think of anyone I've met who doesn't like a chocolate milkshake. With so much goodness in one glass, little can go wrong. Do be sure to chill the glasses, as directed in the first step. A frozen glass is crucial to supreme milkshake enjoyment, which is what we're all ultimately after anyway, right? Right!

Put two 10-ounce glasses in the freezer. Place all of the ingredients in a blender or food processor. Puree until creamy and smooth. Transfer the mixture to the chilled glasses. Serve immediately with straws or long-handled spoons.

makes 2 servings

2 cups chocolate ice cream
½ cup whole milk
1 tablespoon unsweetened
   cocoa powder

FLAVORFUL CHOCOLATE SHAKE ADDITIONS

· 2 tablespoons chocolate hazelnut spread and 1 teaspoon espresso powder
· 2 tablespoons crystallized ginger
· 2 teaspoons lavender buds and 1 teaspoon vanilla extract

Perfect Strawberry Milkshake

makes 2 servings

2 cups vanilla ice cream
½ cup whole milk
½ cup chopped fresh
   strawberries

Over the past few years, I've been amassing a growing collection of straw-berries on our property. At present, we're at thirteen plants. In addition to shortcakes and jam, milkshakes rank high on my list of must-eat straw-berry dishes. While you may be tempted to simply use strawberry ice cream here, do go with the fresh fruits. The juice they impart, especially if just picked, is beyond comparison.

Put two 10-ounce glasses in the freezer. Place all of the ingredients in a blender or food processor. Puree until creamy and smooth. Transfer the mixture to the chilled glasses. Serve immediately with straws or long-handled spoons.

FLAVORFUL STRAWBERRY SHAKE ADDITIONS

- 1 tablespoon minced fresh basil and 1 teaspoon lemon zest
- 1 tablespoon amaretto and 1 tablespoon toasted almond slices
- ¼ cup stewed rhubarb and seeds from ½ vanilla bean pod

Orange Sherbert Shake

If this recipe makes you think of summertime ice cream trucks, then my work here is done. Emblematic of scorching days and long hours spent perfecting my dive at the pool, orange Creamsicles are my unofficial frozen dessert of the hottest season. As so many commercially prepared orange sherberts are laced with artificial ingredients, I've provided a recipe here for creating your own. It takes a bit more time, but the end result is so very worth it.

Begin by making the sherbert. In a medium-size mixing bowl, whisk all of the sherbert ingredients together. Cover the bowl with a lid or plate, and place in the refrigerator to chill for 2 hours.

Place the chilled liquid into an ice cream maker, and prepare according to the manufacturer's instructions. It's ready to be transferred to the freezer when it firms up to the texture of a soft ice cream. Freeze at least two hours before proceeding with the recipe.

Put two 10-ounce glasses in the freezer. Place all of the milkshake ingredients into a blender or food processor. Puree until creamy and smooth. Transfer the mixture to the chilled glasses. Serve immediately with straws or long-handled spoons.

makes 2 servings

1 cup orange sherbert (recipe follows)
1 cup vanilla ice cream
½ cup whole milk
½ cup orange juice

For the Sherbert

½ cup sugar
1 tablespoon orange zest
Pinch of sea salt
1 cup fresh orange juice
1 tablespoon lemon juice
1 teaspoon vanilla extract
1 cup whole milk

Quenched: Orange Sherbert Shake

In 1990 my mother, seemingly out of nowhere, announced to my older brother and me that we'd be moving from our small eastern North Carolina town of Richlands to the emerald shores of the Florida panhandle. While we at first resisted the idea of transitioning somewhere new, leaving friends behind to create new ones—in the early years of high school no less—we soon embraced our geographical shift with enthusiasm. Crashing waves, seagulls, and salty air can do that to a person.

Being a freshman at a new high school where everyone seems to have known each other since kindergarten can be daunting, to say the least. Add in a thriving, competitive, tightly knit athletic department coupled with highly coveted social clubs, and you've got the makings of potential high school nightmares. Fortunately, I quickly found my niche. Signing up for journalism class was my saving grace. There I discovered fellow lovers of word and print, all just as fresh faced and plucky as I was.

To raise money for the journalism department, we held a fundraiser at the local mall. Tucked into the corner of one of its department stores, we students traded shifts after school ended over the course of a week, gift wrapping purchases for a nominal fee. During breaks, I headed out to the food court to grab a bite to eat and something to drink. It was there that I first encountered an Orange Julius. Both a beverage chain and an eponymous drink, the signature Orange Julius consisted of orange juice, milk, sugar, ice, and vanilla. That day, samples of a bit of Julius mixed with vanilla ice cream were being given out, to bring in sales from the curious. I was instantly hooked.

A mere one and a half years after moving to Florida, Mom was ready to leave for somewhere new. In the winter of 1991 we packed a U-Haul truck and set our compass north, to the mountains of western North Carolina. It was hard leaving friends again. Fortunately, those friendships were so formative that they've weathered time and distance, reuniting us online in recent years. That Orange Julius and its fruity, sweet iciness quenched my eager freshman newspaper-staff palate while creating friendships and memories for life.

comforting

Hot chocolate. Say it aloud. Hot chocolate. Your shoulders just relaxed a bit, didn't they? Your mood lightened, right? That's the power of this most comforting of beverages and its kith and kin, hot teas. These immanently sippable delights offer unparalleled pleasure on a chilly day, or when the sniffles hit, or simply when a warming beverage served up in a sturdy mug is what the day calls for.

Decadent Hot Chocolate

*makes 2 to 4
servings*

---

3 cups whole milk
¼ cup good-quality dark
    cocoa powder
2½ ounces good-quality
    baking chocolate (60%
    or higher cocoa content),
    chopped
3 tablespoons sugar
1 tablespoon honey

---

*Few beverages are more comforting on a dreary, cold winter's day than a
warming mug of luscious hot chocolate. Be forewarned, the recipe offered
here is no wimpy cup of cocoa. Far from it. Creamy, rich, thick, this hot
chocolate should feel like a liquid truffle. Adorning with marshmallows is
suggested only for those wishing for a truly decadent experience.*

Warm the milk in a pot over medium-low heat. Add all of the remaining ingredients. Whisk to combine. Continue to whisk over low heat
for 15 minutes, until perfectly creamy and slightly reduced. Serve in 2
large or 4 small mugs.

FLAVORFUL HOT CHOCOLATE ADDITIONS

- *Mayan:* ¼ cup Coffee Liqueur (page 130), a pinch of fresh nutmeg,
  and a pinch of ground cinnamon
- *Citrus:* ¼ teaspoon orange extract and 2 to 4 orange zest strips
- *Minty:* ¼ teaspoon peppermint extract and ¼ cup fresh mint in-
  fused with the milk
- *Caliente:* Pinch of cayenne and ½ teaspoon ground cinnamon

| Lavender Hot Chocolate

makes 1 serving

¼ cup Lavender and Honey
    Ganache (recipe follows)
¾ cup whole milk
Whipped cream or marshmal-
    lows, to serve (optional)
Lavender buds, for garnish
    (optional)

FOR THE LAVENDER AND
HONEY GANACHE

10 ounces dark chocolate
    (65% or higher cocoa
    content; about 2 cups
    when chopped)
3 tablespoons butter, room
    temperature
¼ cup honey
1 cup cream
2 tablespoons lavender buds

Dear friends of ours own and operate a chocolate business in Asheville, North Carolina, called the French Broad Chocolate Lounge. Before they became chocolatiers running one of the hottest dessert cafés in Asheville, Jael and Dan Rattigan could be found surfside in Costa Rica. Ditching law and business school respectively for sunnier shores, the couple gave up books and took on baking, opening a small café in Central America. When their first child was born, they decided to return to the states, bringing a passion for all things cocoa. French Broad Chocolate was born, and I was one of their earliest customers back when they were crafting their sensational confections in their home kitchen. Here they're offering their recipe for Lavender Hot Chocolate. The recipe for the lavender-infused ganache makes enough for several servings, to be enjoyed whenever your chocolate fix needs to be met.

Begin by making the Lavender and Honey Ganache. You can do this one of two ways: on the stovetop or in a food processor.

Stovetop Ganache

Chop the chocolate into small pieces and place in a heatproof bowl. Place the softened butter and honey on top of the chocolate. Set aside.

Heat the cream in a small saucepan over medium-high heat until just boiling. As soon as it reaches a boil, remove the pan from the heat and add the lavender buds. Cover and steep for 10 minutes.

Strain the cream through a fine-mesh sieve set atop a small saucepan. Compost the lavender buds. Place the saucepan over medium-high heat, and bring just to a boil. As soon as it reaches a boil, pour the cream over the chopped chocolate mixture. Let it sit covered for 3 minutes.

Whisk the mixture gently to combine (even better, combine using an immersion blender). As the mixture emulsifies, it will start to take on the appearance of thick pudding. Once all of the chocolate is incorporated, your ganache is ready.

Food Processor Ganache

Heat the cream in a small saucepan over medium-high heat until just boiling. As soon as it reaches a boil, remove the pan from the heat and add the lavender buds. Cover and steep for 10 minutes.

Strain the cream through a fine-mesh sieve set atop a small saucepan. Compost the lavender buds. Place the saucepan over medium-high heat, and bring just to a boil. Remove from the heat.

Chop the chocolate until crumbly in the bowl of the food processor. Add the honey and softened butter. With the machine on, stream in the hot strained lavender cream and process for a few seconds until mostly combined. Stop the machine, and scrape the bowl sides. Process for a few more seconds until mixture is fully emulsified. Scrape into a dish.

Store the lavender and honey ganache in a lidded container in the refrigerator. Use within 1 month.

Hot Chocolate

Place the ganache and milk in a small saucepan over medium heat. Whisk constantly and heat to a simmer. As soon as bubbles begin to emerge at the side of the pan (the French call this "smiling"), it's ready to serve. Pour into a mug. If desired, top with whipped cream or a marshmallow, and garnish with a few lavender buds.

Coconut Hot Chocolate

makes 2 servings

1½ cups Coconut Milk (page 65)

2 tablespoons sugar

3.5-ounce dark chocolate bar (65% or higher cocoa content), chopped

Coconut and chocolate are a natural pairing. Almond Joy, anyone? Yes, please. This liquid rendering of the dynamic duo is a perfect means of treating body and soul on a frosty day. For the daring, consider my optional flavor suggestion below. That bit of curry and lime juice will have you swearing you've replaced your snowy vista with a sun-drenched one.

Place the coconut milk in a medium-size saucepan. Warm over medium heat. Reduce the heat to low just as the milk begins to bubble. Add in the sugar and chocolate. Whisk until the sugar granules are completely dissolved and the chocolate is fully melted. Serve in individual mugs.

FLAVORFUL COCONUT HOT CHOCOLATE ADDITIONS

Add in ½ teaspoon curry powder and a squeeze of fresh lime juice for an added layer of flavor.

Unapologetic Hot Chocolate

If what you like for your hot chocolate is a stand-up-and-say-hello kind of drink, this is the beverage for you. Composed of water, dark chocolate, a bit of sugar, and nothing else, this drink will never make you guess about what's in your mug. Need a justification to imbibe? It would also be a fun means of sampling a variety of chocolate bars, teasing out the cacao notes from various geographic regions.

Place the water in a medium-size saucepan. Bring to a boil over medium-high heat. Reduce the heat to low. Add in the chocolate and sugar. Whisk until the sugar granules are completely dissolved and the chocolate is fully melted. Serve in individual mugs.

makes 2 servings

1¾ cups water

3.5-ounce dark chocolate bar (60% or higher cocoa content), chopped

2 tablespoons sugar

Eggnog Hot Chocolate

3 cups Eggnog (page 180)

1 cup whole milk

3.5-ounce dark chocolate
   bar (60% or higher cocoa
   content), chopped fine

2 tablespoons dark cocoa
   powder

2 tablespoons sugar

Freshly grated nutmeg, to
   your liking

Pinch of salt, if desired

One particularly cold winter's afternoon, as we were gathered around our woodstove, I asked my husband if he'd whip up a batch of his exquisite hot chocolate. Right around the same time, I headed over to the refrigerator, opened it, and looked at a bottle of eggnog I'd recently made. Kismet struck, and the result is the recipe you see here. The flavor of this beverage is pretty much every wonderful thing associated with the holiday and wintertime stretch.

Place the eggnog and milk in a medium-size saucepan. Heat over medium-low heat just until the mixture starts to simmer. Add in the rest of the ingredients. Whisk frequently for about 5 to 8 minutes, until the ingredients are fully incorporated and the mixture has thickened a bit. Cool slightly before serving. The hot chocolate will thicken as it cools.

Quenched: Hot Chocolate

My honeymoon, in early June 2007, was the stuff of fairy tales. After a bit of a whirlwind courtship followed by intense wedding planning, my beloved Glenn and I married on our property June 2 and left two days later for two weeks in Europe. Our itinerary began with five nights in Paris, followed by a day train to Monaco, where we spent four nights in Monte Carlo. After that, an overnight train took us to Rome, where we spent three glorious days eating and walking our way through the Eternal City.

Let me stop for a minute here and say that such jet-setting was not my usual MO. Far from it. I hail from a very humble background, and I felt a bit like I was living someone else's life during that honeymoon. Someone else's life that I very much enjoyed, mind you. My ever-generous in-laws had set up the trip for us and bestowed it upon us as a marriage gift, with the stipulation that we *had* to have the hot chocolate at Angelina in Paris. We readily accepted the mandate, having no clue what Angelina was or why their hot chocolate must be consumed.

I think it was around our third day in the City of Lights that we finally made it to what we learned was one of the most lauded tearooms in all of Paris. Established in 1903 by the Austrian confectioner Antoine Rumpelmayer, Angelina was created as a luxurious destination for the well-heeled traveler to enjoy a pastry and a beverage. We arrived in the late afternoon and were seated with quite possibly the most curmudgeonly server in all of Paris.

Perhaps she'd worked too long a shift, perhaps she was weary of the sight of sweets and happy, blissful children. Whatever it was that had provoked her ire, we received the brunt of it. Fortunately, the hot chocolate we ordered was so thick, and creamy, and rich, and intoxicating, we weren't bothered in the least. We were, after all, on our honeymoon. In Paris. Sipping hot chocolate in a boutique tea shop. It would've been hard to harsh our mellow, even if we were being served by the Parisienne version of the Grinch.

While I have yet to travel back to Paris, whenever I sip a comparable warm mug of hot chocolate, or brew up a cup of my own at home, I'm transported back to those blissful days in Paris when I both quenched my thirst and whetted my appetite for loving companionship.

Chai

makes 2 to 4 servings

---

4 cups cold water

4 to 6 green cardamom pods (see Note)

4 to 6 whole cloves

4 to 6 black peppercorns

2 tablespoons peeled and coarsely chopped fresh ginger

1 tablespoon + 1 teaspoon loose black tea or 3 tea bags (I use Darjeeling)

1 to 2 tablespoons honey

¼ cup whole milk

Defined as "tea," chai is an Indian beverage consisting of black tea, spices, water, and milk. To limit it simply to its component parts, though, doesn't really do it justice, as chai is so, so very much more. Different quantities and selections of spices are used throughout India in creating chai. The one I'm offering here is my bespoke creation. When your morning or afternoon cup of Earl Grey just isn't quite doing it for you, brew a pot of this chai. Its subtle spice and gentle aromas will perk you up in no time.

Add the water and spices to a medium-size saucepan. Bring to a boil over high heat. Reduce the heat to low, place the tea in a tea strainer if using loose (otherwise, add the tea bags), and add it to the pan along with the honey and milk. Simmer for 5 minutes. Remove the pan from the heat. Cover and steep for 5 minutes longer.

Remove and compost the tea. Pour the chai into 2 large mugs or 4 smaller ones. I like to leave the spices in, but you can discard them if you prefer.

Note: The amount of dried spices you opt to use is entirely based on your preferred intensity of flavor. If you like a robust, spice-forward cup of chai, go with 6 each of cardamom pods, whole cloves, and black peppercorns. For something more subtle, select fewer. Either way, you'll need to bruise your cardamom pods before adding them to the water in order to expose the seeds inside. I do this by hitting them with the back of a spoon. Once cracked open, place the whole thing into the pot—pod, seeds, and all.

Decaffeinated Variation

If you love the spicy flavor of chai but would rather forgo the caffeine, simply substitute the tea with an equal amount of either decaffeinated black tea or rooibos tea.

TISANES

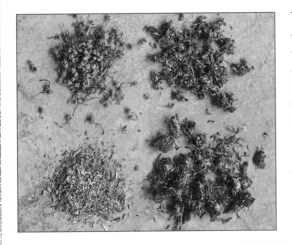

Though often lumped into the same category as their *Camellia sinensis* cousins, "teas" made from herbs are actually not teas at all but instead tisanes. Pronounced "tĭ-zăns," such beverages are made of dried herbs and spices and are typically consumed for their gentle medicinal effects. I've long enjoyed a mug or pot of any number of tisanes when feeling ill or needing a boost. Included here are some of my favorite go-to tisane powerhouses!

Happy Belly Tea

makes ½ cup loose tea, 4 cups prepared

----

3 tablespoons dried spearmint

3 tablespoons dried peppermint

1 tablespoon fennel seeds

1 tablespoon dried tarragon

2 teaspoons dried ginger root
or 1 tablespoon grated
fresh ginger

4 cups boiling water for a full
pot or 1 cup boiling water
for an individual serving

Honey and lemon wedges, to
serve (optional)

Years ago, my stomach and I seemed to always be at odds. No matter what I ate, it fought back, leaving me with more stomachaches than I care to remember. The remedy was easy enough, though. A bit of mint and fennel tea soothed my weary belly in no time. Over time, I learned that tarragon and ginger root expedited healing time and enhanced the flavor, as well.

Place all of the herbs in a mixing bowl. Stir with a spoon to combine.

For a full teapot, place the tea blend in a ceramic or heatproof glass teapot or container. Pour 4 cups of boiling water over the herbs. Cover with a lid, and steep for 15 to 20 minutes. For an individual cup of tea, place 2 tablespoons of tea blend in a teacup and add 1 cup of boiling water. Strain the tea through a fine-mesh sieve. Compost the solids. Alternatively, place the herbs in a mesh tea infuser. Serve as is, or with honey and lemon.

If not using all of the tea right away, store it in an airtight container at room temperature out of direct sunlight. Use within 3 to 4 months.

Throat Soother Tea

A dry, hacking cough does not make for the happiest of days. Give it the heave-ho with this tea. Slippery elm, marshmallow, and licorice are all demulcent herbs, possessing a soothing, mucilaginous quality. Cinnamon and wild cherry are naturally antibacterial, and orange, lemon, and honey impart flavor and sweetness.

Place the herbs and the orange peel in a mixing bowl. Stir with a spoon to combine.

For a full teapot, place the tea blend in a ceramic or heatproof glass teapot or container. Pour 4 cups of boiling water over the herbs. Cover with a lid, and steep for 15 to 20 minutes. For an individual cup of tea, place 2 tablespoons of tea blend in a teacup and add 1 cup of boiling water. Strain the tea through a fine-mesh sieve. Compost the solids. Alternatively, place the herbs in a mesh tea infuser. Serve as is, or with honey and lemon.

If not using all of the tea right away, store it in an airtight container at room temperature out of direct sunlight. Use within 3 to 4 months.

makes ½ cup loose tea, 4 cups prepared

3 tablespoons dried slippery elm bark

3 tablespoons dried marshmallow root

1 tablespoon dried licorice root

One 2-inch cinnamon stick, broken up into pieces

1 teaspoon dried wild cherry bark

1 teaspoon dried orange peel

4 cups boiling water for a full pot or 1 cup boiling water for an individual serving

Honey and lemon wedges, to serve (optional)

Immune Tea

makes ½ cup loose tea, 4 cups prepared

----

3 tablespoons dried lemon
    balm
2 tablespoons dried dandelion
    root
1 tablespoon dried astragalus
    root
2 teaspoons dried ginger root
1 teaspoon dried licorice root
1 teaspoon dried echinacea leaf
1 teaspoon dried rose hips
1 teaspoon dried thyme
4 cups boiling water for a full
    pot or 1 cup boiling water
    for an individual serving
Honey and lemon wedges, to
    serve (optional)

I do not take getting sick sitting down. At the first hint of pain upon swallowing, sniffles, or nasal drip, I fire up the kettle and brew a pot of this tea. The herbs in this blend are detoxifying and immune bolstering, as well as flavorful.

Place all of the herbs in a mixing bowl. Stir with a spoon to combine.

For a full teapot, place the tea blend in a ceramic or heatproof glass teapot or container. Pour 4 cups of boiling water over the herbs. Cover with a lid, and steep for 15 to 20 minutes. For an individual cup of tea, place 2 tablespoons of tea blend in a teacup and add 1 cup boiling water. Strain the tea through a fine-mesh sieve. Compost the solids. Alternatively, place the herbs in a mesh tea infuser. Serve as is, or with honey and lemon.

If not using all of the tea right away, store in an airtight container at room temperature out of direct sunlight. Use within 3 to 4 months.

Women's Fertili-Tea

Whether or not you are attempting to conceive, this tea is wonderful for women. Red clover, red raspberry leaf, and nettle leaf are nourishing and balancing to female reproductive health. There's a long steeping time, so I like to make this upon first rising. Alternatively, you can steep it before going to bed at night. It's equally delicious served hot, with lemon and honey, or cold, with ice.

Place the dried herbs in a ceramic teapot or heatproof glass container. Pour the boiling water over them, and cover with a lid. Leave to steep for 2 to 4 hours. Strain the tea through a fine-mesh sieve. Compost the solids. Alternatively, place the herbs in a mesh tea infuser. Serve as is, or with honey and lemon.

If not consumed immediately, store in a lidded container in the refrigerator. Use within 3 to 4 days.

makes 4 cups / 1 serving

2 tablespoons dried red clover buds

2 tablespoons dried red raspberry leaves

2 tablespoons dried nettle leaves

4 cups boiling water

Honey and lemon wedges, to serve (optional)

Quenched: Women's Fertili-Tea

Many years ago, in my early twenties, I worked as the bulk herbs and spices buyer for Whole Foods in Arlington, Virginia. Filling those jars with licorice root twigs or fluffy bits of marshmallow root or intoxicating green cardamom pods brought me happiness that was, and still is, hard to fully describe. Something about the trinity of tactile, olfactory, and visual qualities those bits of dried plant matter presented intoxicated and enthralled me.

Wanting to learn more about what it was they all did, I scoured books for information and enthusiastically looked forward to the in-store training sessions from the lines of herbal medicinal products the store carried. Later, after relocating to Asheville, North Carolina, I went on to take numerous classes in herbalism offered in the area, as well as attend local conferences on herbs and healing. If it was herbal, I was in.

It stood to reason, then, that after marrying and discussing beginning a family with my husband, herbs would come into play. Having never been pregnant before, I wasn't even sure if I could conceive, let alone carry a pregnancy to term. Herbs had been my constant companion for health needs for over a decade at that point, and I knew they'd be essential in my journey toward motherhood.

During research on herbs suggested for enhancing fertility, I found advice from the renowned herbalist Susun Weed. She suggested a blend of various herbs, including some amounts of red clover, red raspberry leaf, and nettles, among other things. I decided I'd give it a try and purchased a pound of each. The recipe provided here is what I created, and then I committed to consuming a quart of it daily for one year.

Whether or not it was the herbal tea blend, or serendipity, or mental readiness, or what have you, I became pregnant on the second attempt. I have since gone on to recommend this tea to numerous friends of mine wanting to start families of their own. I'm not a doctor or an herbalist, so I can't make any medical claims to efficacy except for my own. That said, this tea quenched my intense desire to begin a family and furthered my love of all things herbal and healing. There's also the fact that every girlfriend I suggested it to has since gone on to become a mother. Oh, the glorious healing, green goodness of herbs. I'll drink to that!

GUEST RECIPE | Pleasant Dreams Tea

Nicole McConville is my editor at Lark Books. She and I have worked together on five books, our personal friendship deepening right alongside our professional one. This recipe is her blend for overcoming insomnia. As she tells it: "This is my personal go-to remedy for calming the overactive mind that stems from our overly connected, staring-too-long-at-too-many-screens lifestyle. Chamomile, long celebrated for its relaxant and sedative properties, will help you slow down for the night. Kava kava steadies the nerves. Passionflower helps to ease cyclical thinking (the kind that happens to keep you up in the wee hours). Oat straw helps ease anxiety and stress. Orange rind and cinnamon are added simply to sweeten things up a bit. I like to add a big spoonful of local wildflower honey for even more of a palatable finish."

amount varies

Equal parts herbs (see Note):
  Chamomile
  Kava kava
  Passionflower
  Oat straw
  Orange peel (dried preferred)
  Cinnamon (chips preferred)

Combine equal parts of each ingredient in a large bowl until well blended. Fill a tea ball or tea bag and put it in a cup. Top with boiling water. Steep for at least a few minutes, covered. Sip while hot. I find it's best to drink this tea every night approximately half an hour before I want to go to bed.

If not using all of the tea right away, store it in an airtight container at room temperature out of direct sunlight. Use within 3 to 4 months.

Note: Most health stores will have chamomile available for sale. If you cannot find kava kava or passionflower locally, it is widely available through herbal companies. My favorite is Mountain Rose Herbal, celebrated for its organic and sustainably sourced materials.

When determining quantities, note that a teaspoon of each herb will make a small batch that yields just a few servings; ½ cup of each herb will make a larger batch you can keep on hand or gift.

Warning: If you have allergies to plants in the ragweed family avoid this tea. If you have any liver issues at all, remove the kava kava and substitute that measurement with an equal amount of additional chamomile. This tea should not be consumed by pregnant women unless the kava kava and passionflower are removed.

HARD DRINKS

TODDIES, LIQUEURS, WINES, CIDERS, CORDIALS, BITTERS, PUNCHES—THE BOLD, ENLIVENING, STIMULATING DRINKS FOUND WITHIN THIS SECTION FALL INTO THE BEVERAGE ARENA REFERRED TO AS "HARD" DRINKS. FROM A PITCHER OF SEASONAL FRUIT—IMBUED SANGRIA TO A COCKTAIL LACED WITH CRÈME DE MENTHE, THESE DRINKS SHINE EQUALLY BRIGHT WHETHER QUAFFED IN FESTIVE COMPANY OR SIPPED SOLO. CRAFT A BEVERAGE, GATHER YOUR NEAREST AND DEAREST, AND RAISE A GLASS IN CELEBRATION. CHEERS!

spirited

Tipple. Hooch. Booze. Firewater. No matter what you call it, here we're talking about the stuff that lowers inhibitions and relaxes weary bodies. The beverages in this section were created using the freshest ingredients available to render cleaner, more natural variations of popular alcoholic beverages. I'm a big fan of cocktail hour, daily, and wanted to craft drinks for friends, family, and the world at large that I could feel good about serving—and swilling. I raise my glass to you in tribute!

How to Infuse Liquor

Crafting homemade infused liquors couldn't be easier. Alcohol and infusing ingredients are combined, set aside while their flavors meld, strained, bottled, and stored. It really is that simple! In the following pages, I offer recipes for infusing vodka, rum, brandy, and whiskey. The alcohol you're using will determine how long the alcohol steeps and where it's stored once finished.

Vodka and rum

After combining the vodka or rum and other ingredients, set aside the bottle to infuse in a cool, dark place such as a pantry or lower cabinet for one week. Check the flavor. If you prefer a stronger flavor, leave the mix to infuse an additional week. Using a fine-mesh sieve, coffee filter, or fine cheesecloth, strain the liquor into a bowl. Compost the solids. Using a funnel, transfer the infusion back to the jar used for processing (after cleaning it out) or into a decorative bottle for gifting. Store according to recipe instructions.

Brandy

After combining the brandy and other ingredients, set aside the bottle to infuse in a cool, dark place such as a pantry or lower cabinet for one week. Using a fine-mesh sieve, coffee filter, or fine cheesecloth, strain the liquor into a bowl. Compost the solids. Transfer the infusion back to the jar used for processing and leave to infuse an additional two weeks. Strain off the liquor using fine cheesecloth or siphon with a turkey baster, taking care to avoid any debris at the bottom of the bottle. Using a funnel, transfer the liquor to a clean bottle. Store according to recipe instructions.

Whiskey

After combining the whiskey and other ingredients, set aside the bottle to infuse in a cool, dark place such as a pantry or lower cabinet for three days. Check the flavor. If you prefer a stronger flavor, leave the mix to infuse an additional two days. Using a fine-mesh sieve, coffee filter, or fine cheesecloth, strain the liquor into a bowl. Compost the solids. Using a funnel, transfer the infusion back to the jar used for processing (after cleaning it out) or into a decorative bottle for gifting. Store according to recipe instructions.

Basil Vodka

Vodka infused with the aromatic oils of fresh basil leaves capitalizes on the wonder of this iconic summertime herb. It complements gimlets expertly and would be most welcome in a Bloody Mary.

Place the basil leaves in a clean and dry quart-size glass container with an airtight lid (such as a Mason jar). Cover the leaves with the vodka, and secure the lid tightly. Follow the instructions on page 104 for infusing the vodka.

Store the infusion in the refrigerator, and use within 1 month; or store it in the freezer, and use within 2 months.

Hot Pepper Vodka

This vodka is for those who like a bit of heat with their hooch. Use it in martinis with a bit of vermouth and a bit of olive juice for a cocktail with high-kicking legs.

Place the peppers in a clean and dry quart-size glass container with an airtight lid (such as a Mason jar). Cover with the vodka, and secure the lid tightly. Follow the instructions on page 104 for infusing the vodka.

Store the infusion in the refrigerator, and use within 1 month; or store it in the freezer, and use within 2 months.

Cranberry Vodka

makes 3¼ cups

1 cup fresh cranberries
One 750-ml bottle medium-
    quality vodka

Cranberry vodka is a wonderful means of employing all those ruby-hued orbs that appear but for an ephemeral period come wintertime. In tandem with enjoying the berries in their traditional sauced style at holiday meals, sip on a cranberry vodka Cosmopolitan or cranberry vodka on the rocks with sparkling water and cranberry juice.

Place the cranberries in a clean and dry quart-size glass container with an airtight lid (such as a Mason jar). Cover with the vodka, and secure the lid tightly. Follow the instructions on page 104 for infusing the vodka.

Store the infusion in the refrigerator, and use within 1 month; or store it in the freezer, and use within 2 months.

Vanilla Vodka

makes 3¼ cups

2 fresh vanilla beans
One 750-ml bottle medium-
    quality vodka

Having a bottle of vanilla vodka at the ready comes in handy in a variety of culinary arenas. Mix it with a bit of Cola (page 18) or Orange Soda (page 20) for a refreshing thirst quencher on a hot day, combine it in a chilled glass with some Amaretto (page 129) for an after-dinner drink, or place it in individual bottles with whole vanilla beans for homemade vanilla extract.

Using a fine-tipped knife, slice open the vanilla bean pods from top to bottom. Place the bean pods in a clean and dry quart-size glass container with an airtight lid (such as a Mason jar). Cover with the vodka, and secure the lid tightly. Follow the instructions on page 104 for infusing the vodka.

Store the infusion in the refrigerator, and use within 1 month; or store it in the freezer, and use within 2 months.

Coconut Rum

Sometime in the mid-1990s, I dressed up as Molly Ringwald and headed to an '80s party. When I arrived, the drink of choice was uncompromisingly girly, tropical, and almost dangerously easy to drink. Combine pineapple juice, Amaretto (page 129), and coconut rum to fashion an "Italian Surfer," and watch your scrunchy-haired, frosted-lipsticked, Members Only–jacketed cares drift away.

makes 3¼ cups

1 fresh coconut
One 750-ml bottle medium-
    quality white or light rum

Begin by prepping the coconut. Using either a screwdriver or a drill, punch a hole in one of the eyes of the coconut. Drain the liquid inside, and set it aside to drink later. Place the whole coconut in a large sealable freezer bag. Throw the bag against a hard surface, such as your kitchen floor or, even better, a cement floor, if you have one. You're trying to crack open the coconut here, so give it a hard throw and repeat as needed until it breaks into pieces.

Using a small, sharp knife (and a great deal of caution), separate the shell from the coconut flesh. With a vegetable peeler, peel away the brown skin adhering to the flesh. Rinse under cool water, and pat dry with a kitchen cloth.

Place the coconut in a clean and dry ½-gallon glass container with an airtight lid (such as a Mason jar). Cover with the rum, and secure the lid tightly. Follow the instructions on page 104 for infusing the rum.

Store the infusion in the refrigerator, and use within 1 month; or store it in the freezer, and use within 2 months.

Spiced Rum

makes 3¼ cups

4 whole cloves

4 allspice berries

4 black peppercorns

4 green cardamom pods,
    gently bruised

One 2-inch cinnamon stick

Peel from 1 orange (see Note)

One 750-ml bottle medium-
    quality aged rum

This rum is the stuff of very good times. I like adding a generous lashing of it to Eggnog (page 180) or tipping a healthy jigger into a bit of Cola (page 18). It's also always welcome come holiday time and makes for a great gift. Plan ahead, though, as you'll need several weeks of steeping before it's ready to bottle.

Place the spices and orange peel in a clean and dry quart-size glass container with an airtight lid (such as a Mason jar). Cover with the rum, and secure the lid tightly. Follow the instructions on page 104 for infusing the rum.

   Store in a dark, cool, dry place, and use within 1 year.

Note: Use a vegetable peeler to remove the orange peel, taking care to avoid any white pith.

Pineapple Rum

This is the rum you should be drinking when the mercury soars. Mix it with a bit of Lemon Lime Soda (page 23) and pineapple juice, or combine it with mint and sparkling water for an invigorating mojito. Whatever use you ultimately put it to, know that it will be unequivocally delicious.

Begin by prepping the pineapple. Chop off the leafy top, peel the sides, and remove the hard core. Cut the peeled and cored pineapple in half vertically. Set aside one half to eat later. Cut the remaining half into four spears.

Place the pineapple spears in a clean and dry ½-gallon glass container with an airtight lid (such as a Mason jar). Cover with the rum, and secure the lid tightly. Follow the instructions on page 104 for infusing the rum.

Store the infusion in the refrigerator, and use within 1 month; or store it in the freezer, and use within 2 months.

makes 3¼ cups

1 fresh pineapple
One 750-ml bottle medium-
    quality white or light rum

Pear Brandy

makes 3¼ cups

2 medium-size firm yet ripe
    pears
One 750-ml bottle medium-
    quality brandy

For several years, I spent a number of summer and autumn days and evenings helping my friend Jessica Gregory with her sustainable wedding floral design business, Aria Floral. Jessica often decorated tables with edible elements, including seasonal fruits and vegetables. When the weddings were done, she took all of that fresh produce home, cooking up the veggies and creating brandies with the fruit. This brandy always makes me think of her. It's glorious on its own in a snifter (a crackling warm fire in the background is highly recommended) and would also be lovely topped off with sparkling wine or tucked into a mug of warm apple cider.

Slice the pears into quarters. Discard the stems and seeds. Place the pear segments in a clean and dry ½-gallon glass container with an airtight lid (such as a Mason jar). Cover with the brandy, and secure the lid tightly. Follow the instructions on page 104 for infusing the brandy.

Store in a dark, cool, dry place, and use within 1 year.

Stone Fruit Brandy

makes 3¼ cups

3 medium-size stone fruits,
    including a mixture of
    peaches, nectarines,
    plums, apricots, and
    pluots
One 750-ml bottle medium-
    quality brandy

When the stone fruits of summer are at their peak, set aside a few for brandy. Select fruits with both a bit of give when gently pressed and a detectable aroma, two telltale indications of ripeness. Enjoy this brandy on the rocks with a bit of Peach Nectar (page 29) and sparkling water, or nestled into a hot cup of coffee on a chilly winter's night when the sunny days of summer are but a distant memory.

Slice the stone fruits into quarters. Remove and compost their stones. Place the fruit segments in a clean and dry ½-gallon glass container with an airtight lid (such as a Mason jar). Cover with the brandy, and secure the lid tightly. Follow the instructions on page 104 for infusing the brandy.

Store in a dark, cool, dry place, and use within 1 year.

Blackberry Brandy

makes 3¼ cups

1 cup blackberries
One 750-ml bottle medium-
    quality brandy

The summer of 2008, I left my stable, paying job. Taking a colossal leap of faith, I left the comfort of nine-to-five life for one following my own time schedule, wherein wearing PJs to "work" is not only acceptable but encouraged. Serendipitously, an offer to pen a book series on topics I was quite familiar with presented itself. Before beginning to write, though, I enjoyed a few brief weeks of excessive loafing, lounging, and reading. The novels of Joanne Harris (of Chocolat *fame) filled my humid days.* Blackberry Wine *was the first I read, detailing the recollections of a man seeking answers to childhood questions. Whenever I think of blackberries now, in any form, I think of those novels, and those interstitial days. This brandy is sensational on its own and would be wonderful muddled with some fresh berries, apple juice, and a bit of sparkling water.*

Place the blackberries in a clean and dry quart-size glass container with an airtight lid (such as a Mason jar). Cover with the brandy, and secure the lid tightly. Follow the instructions on page 104 for infusing the brandy.

Store in a dark, cool, dry place, and use within 1 year.

Apple Brandy

makes 3¼ cups

2 sweet apples
One 750-ml bottle medium-
    quality brandy

My favorite season by far is autumn. Its riot of foliage color, smell of smoke and cinders, and opportunities for donning scarves and cardigans are balms for my hot weather–weary soul. This brandy heightens the season's unofficial mascot, apples. Add a bit to a chilled glass with sparkling apple juice, or mix it into a hot cup of Earl Grey tea for a bit of autumnal bliss.

Slice the apples into quarters. Discard the stems and seeds. Place the apple segments in a clean and dry quart-size glass container with an airtight lid (such as a Mason jar). Cover with the brandy, and secure the lid tightly. Follow the instructions on page 104 for infusing the brandy.

Store in a dark, cool, dry place, and use within 1 year.

Orange and Clove Whiskey

When it's toddy-making time, make this your go-to whiskey of choice. One glug of this, a warm blanket, and a riveting read are all you need to chase away any cool-weather chill.

Place the cloves and orange peel in a clean and dry quart-size glass container with an airtight lid (such as a Mason jar). Cover with the whiskey, and secure the lid tightly. Follow the instructions on page 104 for infusing the whiskey.

Store in a dark, cool, dry place, and use within 1 year.

Note: Use a vegetable peeler to remove the orange peel, taking care to avoid the white pith.

makes 3¼ cups

4 whole cloves
Peel from 1 orange (see Note)
One 750-ml bottle
    good-quality whiskey

Black and Blue Whiskey

If an annual pilgrimage to the U-pick berry farm isn't on your agenda, it should be. Plucking fresh berries from their bramble or bush and into your collecting basket—and the ink-stained fingers it results in—is one of life's abiding pleasures, I've long maintained. This whiskey puts your hard work to good use. Come imbibing time, mix a bit with Cola (page 18) or tuck into a mug of hot coffee for a smooth-sipping reminder of the joys of summer.

makes 3¼ cups

¼ cup blackberries
¼ cup blueberries
One 750-ml bottle
   good-quality whiskey

Place the berries in a clean and dry quart-size glass container with an airtight lid (such as a Mason jar). Cover with the whiskey, and secure the lid tightly. Follow the instructions on page 104 for infusing the whiskey.

Store in a dark, cool, dry place, and use within 1 year.

Fig and Vanilla Whiskey

For a new twist on a classic, try this whiskey in a sour. The subtle sweetness of the fruit is a nice foil to the drink's characteristic puckeryness. It would also be lovely poured over fruitcake during its soaking period.

makes 3¼ cups

8 fresh ripe figs
1 vanilla bean
One 750-ml bottle
   good-quality whiskey

Slice the figs in half, removing any stems. Using a fine-tipped knife, slice the vanilla bean pod open from top to bottom. Place the figs and vanilla bean in a clean and dry quart-size glass container with an airtight lid (such as a Mason jar). Cover with the whiskey, and secure the lid tightly. Follow the instructions on page 104 for infusing the whiskey.

Store in a dark, cool, dry place, and use within 1 year.

Cinnamon and Apple Whiskey

makes 3¼ cups

½ cup dried apple pieces
One 2-inch cinnamon stick
One 750-ml bottle
    good-quality whiskey

If asked to describe the flavors of autumn, I'd imagine cinnamon and apples would warrant repeat mention by most. An ideal pairing if there ever was one, the spice and fruit perfectly complement each other. Enjoy this whiskey on the rocks with a bit of vermouth or spiked into a mug of hot apple cider.

Place the dried apple slices and cinnamon stick in a clean and dry quart-size glass container with an airtight lid (such as a Mason jar). Cover with the whiskey, and secure the lid tightly. Follow the instructions on page 104 for infusing the whiskey.

Store in a dark, cool, dry place, and use within 1 year.

Pear Liqueur

The first time I tasted real eau-de-vie de poire, *a pear liqueur, I was astonished by its profound deliciousness. The clear liquid belies the perfumed bouquet it possesses. It's not easy to find, though, and instead of attempting to ferment and then distill my own (which is laborious and illegal), I instead turned to making pear liqueur. By simply infusing ripe pears with a bit of lemon peel and cloves in vodka, the pleasures of pear liqueur can soon be yours. Serve small glasses chilled for a real treat. It's also wonderful topped off with champagne or sparkling wine.*

Peel the pears, and slice them into thin pieces. Discard the stems and seeds. Place the pear slices, lemon peel, and cloves in a clean and dry quart-size glass container with an airtight lid (such as a Mason jar). Cover with the vodka, and secure the lid tightly. Store the jar in a cool, dark area out of direct sunlight, such as a pantry or bottom cabinet, for 1 week. Give the container a shake whenever you think of it.

Place the infusion in a mixing bowl. Mash the pears with a metal spoon, bruising and breaking them up a bit. Strain the liqueur through either a fine-mesh wire strainer, coffee filter, or cheesecloth placed atop a bowl. Compost the solids.

Transfer the infusion back to the jar used for processing (after cleaning it out) or into a decorative bottle for gifting. Store in a dark, cool, dry place, and consume within 1 year.

makes 3¼ cups

4 medium-size firm yet ripe pears
Peel from 1 lemon
6 whole cloves
One 750-ml bottle 80 or 100 proof medium-quality vodka

Cherry Liqueur

makes 4 cups

Simple syrup (recipe follows)
1 pound sweet cherries,
    stemmed and pitted
    (reserve pits)
2 cups vodka
2 cups brandy

FOR THE *SIMPLE SYRUP*

1½ cups sugar
1 cup water

While not typically a bar staple, the appearance of cherry liqueur enhances the contents of a cocktail considerably. Mix a bit with gin and a dash of lemon juice, or Spiced Rum (page 110) and orange juice, for cocktails reaching beyond the usual and expected.

Combine the sugar and water in a small saucepan to make a simple syrup. Bring to a boil, stirring until all of the sugar granules have fully dissolved. Remove from the heat. Cool to room temperature.

Place the cherries, reserved pits, cooled simple syrup, vodka, and brandy in a ½-gallon glass container. Cover with a lid, give a good shake, and leave to infuse in a cool, dark location such as a kitchen pantry or bottom cabinet for 3 weeks.

Strain the liqueur through a fine-mesh sieve placed atop a bowl. Compost the solids. Return the liquid to the jar, and put it back in its infusing location for an additional 2 weeks. Strain the liqueur again through a cheesecloth-lined sieve placed atop a bowl or by siphoning the liqueur with a turkey baster, leaving any debris at the bottom of the container.

Transfer the infusion back to the jar used for processing (after cleaning it out) or into a decorative bottle for gifting. Store in the refrigerator, and consume within 3 to 4 months.

GUEST RECIPE | Limoncello

makes four 750-ml bottles

Zest from 15 to 20 organic lemons (about 2 to 3 cups)

Two 750-ml bottles high-proof pure grain alcohol (or vodka)

Simple syrup (recipe follows)

FOR THE SIMPLE SYRUP

6 cups water

4 cups sugar

Linda Ly, the voice behind the award-winning blog Garden Betty, *is no shrinking violet. While her nights are spent clicking on her keyboard as a freelance designer, her days are lived to the fullest, whether she's surfing, kayaking, climbing, camping, snowboarding, skiing, gardening, baking, cooking, or otherwise moving about. Her recipe for Limoncello, shared here, first caught my eye when it appeared on* Garden Betty *several years ago. Linda's emphasis on fresh, natural, slow, loving food preparation speaks my culinary language, and her enthusiasm for life is absolutely infectious. Salute!*

Thoroughly wash and scrub the lemons to remove any dirt or residue from the skins. Dry them completely. Zest all the lemons, taking care to remove only the yellow outer layer of skin and not the white pith underneath (which can make your Limoncello taste bitter).

Pour the alcohol and zest into a 1-gallon glass jar, and secure the lid tightly. Keep the jar in a cool, dark place, and let the lemon zest steep for at least 3 weeks if using pure grain alcohol or up to 6 weeks if using vodka. The alcohol will take on a bright yellow hue during this time. You'll know the lemon zest has released all of its oils when the shreds turn white and brittle.

In a medium saucepan, make a simple syrup by bringing the water and sugar to a slow boil. Stir until the sugar is dissolved, then remove from the heat and let the syrup cool. Add the simple syrup to your jar of lemon-infused alcohol, stir to combine, and secure the lid tightly again. Let the mixture sit for at least 1 week; the Limoncello will mellow out a lot during this period. It gets smoother the longer it ages, so try to resist the urge to bottle it right away and let it age for 2 weeks or more.

Strain the Limoncello through a fine-mesh sieve to remove all the zest. Then, strain the Limoncello again using an ultrafine-mesh sieve, coffee filter, or cheesecloth to remove any remaining pulp and zest. You want the liqueur to be as clear as possible. This second straining can be funneled directly into the final bottles. If you're making this just for yourself, you can reuse the original bottles of alcohol or even clean wine bottles.

Taste the Limoncello. If you prefer it sweeter, you can add a bit more simple syrup. Just keep in mind that the flavor continues to mellow out over time, so if you don't plan to drink the bottles for a few months, let them age and do a final tasting later.

Limoncello is best served chilled, so store your bottles in the freezer (along with a set of cordial glasses), and you'll always be ready for dessert!

Irish Cream

A longtime lover of Irish cream, it stood to reason I'd eventually learn to make my own. Not only is it considerably less expensive to do so; it also eliminates the artificial ingredients and preservatives used in commercially prepared options. Whip up a batch of this creamy goodness come holiday time and get ready to accept the hearty embraces and thankful pats on the back this beverage elicits. It's that good. Fabulous on its own with ice, it is equally lovely served with coffee.

Place the coffee in a medium-size saucepan. Bring to a gentle simmer. Add the cream, cocoa, sugar, honey, and extracts. Whisk thoroughly until all ingredients are fully combined. Reduce the heat to low, and simmer for 20 minutes, whisking frequently, until the mixture begins to thicken. Remove the saucepan from the heat, and whisk in the sweetened condensed milk. Transfer the mixture to a heatproof glass or ceramic bowl, and set aside to cool for a few minutes. Whisk in the whiskey until completely blended.

At this point, you can either allow the mixture to cool to room temperature and then serve it or transfer it to a lidded container and store it in the refrigerator. Serve in individual glasses over ice. If not consumed right away, use within 7 to 10 days.

Note: The sweetened condensed milk I use includes only organic milk and sugar. If you'd rather make your own, bear in mind that you'll need to allocate several hours for reducing the milk before you're able to proceed with the rest of the recipe.

makes 4 cups

1 cup strong brewed coffee

1½ cups heavy cream

1 tablespoon dark cocoa powder

1 tablespoon sugar

1 teaspoon honey

½ teaspoon vanilla extract

½ teaspoon almond extract

One 14-ounce can sweetened condensed milk (see Note)

2 cups Irish whiskey

Crème de Menthe

1 cup fresh mint leaves
1½ cups vodka
Simple syrup (recipe follows)

FOR THE *SIMPLE SYRUP*

1 cup sugar
2 cups water

If you enjoy the occasional "adult" hot chocolate redolent of peppermint canes, come holiday time, this is the beverage for you. To that end, this treat makes a wonderful gift, especially if wrapped up with all-natural peppermint sticks and homemade marshmallows. It's also wonderful served shaken with ice and heavy cream.

Coarsely chop the mint leaves. Place the mint in a clean and dry ½-gallon glass container with an airtight lid (such as a Mason jar). Pour the vodka over the mint, and secure the lid tightly. Set aside to infuse in a cool, dark location such as a kitchen pantry or bottom cabinet for 1 week. Strain the liquid through a fine-mesh sieve set atop a bowl. Compost the solids. Return the vodka infusion to the sealable container.

Combine the sugar and water in a small saucepan. Bring to a boil, stirring until all of the sugar granules have fully dissolved. Remove from the heat. Cool to room temperature. Add the simple syrup to the vodka, and give the container a good shake to combine. Store in the refrigerator, and use within 3 to 4 months.

Amaretto

I will forever associate amaretto with my mother in the early 1980s. Clad in skin-tight Gloria Vanderbilt jeans, hair feathered à la Farrah Fawcett, and perpetually listening to the Eagles or a young Rod Stewart, my mother's drink of choice was amaretto. When I learned just how easy it is to make your own, and that many commercially prepared offerings include caramel coloring, I abandoned the liquor store and turned to my pantry. If you intend to gift this drink, bear in mind that it needs four weeks for its initial steeping period, followed by an additional two weeks of settling. Serve neat, on the rocks, with coffee, or in a sour.

Place the almonds, vodka, brandy, apricots, and lemon zest in a clean and dry ½-gallon glass container with an airtight lid (such as a Mason jar). Cover with a lid, and give it a good shake. Store the jar in a cool, dark area out of direct sunlight, such as a kitchen pantry or bottom cabinet, for 4 weeks. Give the container a shake whenever you think of it.

Using either a fine-mesh strainer, coffee filter, or cheesecloth, strain the liqueur into a bowl. Repeat this process, allowing as much time as necessary for the liquid to fully strain off (this may take several hours). Compost the solids.

Meanwhile, combine the brown sugar and water in a small saucepan to make a simple syrup. Bring it to a boil, stirring until all of the sugar granules have fully dissolved. Remove it from the heat. Cool it to room temperature.

Rinse and dry the container used in infusing. Return the liqueur to it, and add the cooled simple syrup and extracts. Give the container a good shake to combine. Return the jar to its infusing location for an additional 2 weeks. Strain the liqueur one final time using a cheesecloth-lined sieve placed atop a bowl or by siphoning it off with a turkey baster, leaving any debris at the bottom of the container. Store in a dark, cool, dry place, and consume within 6 months.

makes 4 cups

2 cups raw almonds, coarsely chopped

1½ cups vodka

1½ cups brandy

⅓ cup dried apricots, coarsely chopped

Zest from 1 medium-size lemon

Simple syrup (recipe follows)

2 teaspoons almond extract

2 teaspoons vanilla extract

For the Simple Syrup

1 cup dark brown sugar

½ cup water

Coffee Liqueur

makes 5 cups

2 cups boiling water

½ cup finely ground Arabica
    coffee beans

Simple syrup (recipe follows)

2 tablespoons vanilla extract

2 cups light rum

FOR THE SIMPLE SYRUP

2 cups light brown sugar

1 cup water

The 1998 comedy The Big Lebowski, *written and directed by Joel and Ethan Coen, forever etched a love of coffee liqueur in my mind. The unemployed, unconcerned, unforgettable title character (who refers to himself simply as "The Dude") deftly portrayed by Jeff Bridges shares a deep love of White Russians, in which coffee liqueur plays a central role. Put on your favorite fluffy robe, trade your loafers for slippers, combine a bit of this liqueur with some vodka and cream, and allow your inner Dude to abide.*

Place the ground coffee in a French press or small bowl. Pour the boiling water over the grounds, and steep for 5 minutes. If using a French press, depress the plunger. If using a small bowl, pour the liquid through a fine-mesh sieve set atop a bowl. Set aside.

Meanwhile, combine the brown sugar and water in a small saucepan to make a simple syrup. Bring it to a boil, stirring until all of the sugar granules have fully dissolved. Remove from the heat. Cool to room temperature.

In a sealable glass container, combine the cooled coffee and simple syrup. Add the vanilla extract and rum. Cover with a lid, give a good shake, and store in a cool, dark area, such as a kitchen pantry or bottom cabinet, for 4 weeks. Store in a cool, dark, dry place, and use within 3 to 4 months.

Vin Maison Spring and Summer

1 cup chopped peaches,
    nectarines, or plums (or a
    mixture of the three) or 1
    cup strawberries, black-
    berries, or raspberries (or
    a mixture of the three)
3 tablespoons sugar
¼ cup vodka
One 750-ml bottle white wine
    (such as Sauvignon Blanc
    or Pinot Grigio)
Ice or sparkling water, to serve
    (optional)

House wine, or vin maison, *is perhaps my favorite French creation (although the Louvre certainly is nice, as are baguettes). Enjoyed in cafés and homes throughout the country during the postwork, not-yet-dinner period known as* apéritif *(referring to both the event and the beverage itself), vin maison is a blend of wine, some liquor, a bit of sugar, and whatever fruits and herbs are seasonally available. Fresh stone fruits in summer or berries in late spring/early summer produce a delicious means of transitioning from the business of the workday to the leisure of home and family time. Santé!*

Combine the fruits, sugar, vodka, and white wine in a clean and dry ½-gallon glass container with an airtight lid (such as a Mason jar). Stir until the sugar granules are fully dissolved. Secure with a lid, give a good shake, and store in the refrigerator for 3 weeks.

Strain the liquid through a cheesecloth-lined sieve set atop a bowl. Use a spoon to press down on the fruit to extract as much liquid as possible. Compost the solids. Transfer the wine to a lidded container. Store in the refrigerator. To serve, pour about ½ cup into an 8-ounce glass. Serve with ice, sparkling water, or plain. Use within 1 to 2 months.

Vin Maison Autumn and Winter

This vin maison is for the chillier times of year. A bit of cinnamon, cloves, and star anise imbue the wine with heat and warmth. Bear in mind that the wine needs ample time to infuse, so plan to have bottles regularly steeping in the refrigerator if you'd like to routinely enjoy this aperitif.

Combine the fruits, sugar, vodka, spices, and red wine in a clean and dry ½-gallon glass container with an airtight lid (such as a Mason jar). Stir until the sugar granules are fully dissolved. Secure with a lid, give a good shake, and store in the refrigerator for 3 weeks.

Strain the liquid through a cheesecloth-lined sieve set atop a bowl. Use a spoon to press down on the fruit to extract as much liquid as possible. Compost the solids. Transfer the wine to a lidded container. Store in the refrigerator. To serve, pour about ½ cup into an 8-ounce glass. Serve with ice, sparkling water, or plain. Use within 1 to 2 months.

makes 3¼ cups

1 cup chopped apples or pears
(or a combination of the two)

3 tablespoons sugar

¼ cup vodka

One 2-inch cinnamon stick

4 whole cloves

1 star anise

One 750-ml bottle red wine
(such as Pinot Noir or
Malbec)

Ice or sparking water, to serve
(optional)

GUEST RECIPE | Elderflower Liqueur

makes 2 cups

15 elderflower heads
Simple syrup (recipe follows)
1 lemon
Vodka and sparkling water, or
    sparkling wine, to serve

For the *Simple Syrup*

2½ cups water
2 cups sugar

My friend Barbara Swell is a culinary Renaissance woman. A cookbook author, she also teaches antique cooking lessons year-round in a log cabin situated adjacent to her home, gardens, bakes (Swell holds a much-loved annual Retro Pie Contest), hosts parties, and engages in every food-based pursuit I know of. She graciously shared her recipe for Elderflower Liqueur with me, as I recently learned my one-mile dirt driveway is flanked by the native bushes. Do be sure to pick the flowers on a dry day, as wetness both dampens their subtle flavor and invites spoilage.

Gently brush any bugs off the elderflowers. Using kitchen scissors, snip off any green stems or leaves, leaving only the flowers. Place in a medium-size glass or ceramic bowl.

Combine the water and sugar in a small saucepan to make a simple syrup. Bring to a boil, stirring until all of the sugar granules have fully dissolved. Remove from the heat. Cool to room temperature.

Using a vegetable peeler, remove the zest from the lemon in wide strips. Take care to avoid removing any white pith with the peel. Slice the peeled lemon into thin rings, removing any seeds.

Pour the cooled simple syrup over the elderflowers. Add the lemon slices and lemon zest. Stir gently with a metal spoon to combine. Cover the bowl with a plate or lid. Leave at room temperature for 24 hours. Strain the liquid through a fine-mesh sieve set atop a bowl. Compost the solids.

Store in a clean glass container in the refrigerator. To serve, add 1 to 2 tablespoons to a glass and top with sparkling wine or 2 ounces of vodka and sparkling water. Use within 2 to 3 weeks, or freeze for up to 6 months.

Rhubarb Bitters (Spring)

makes 3 cups

1 cup chopped rhubarb

Zest from 2 lemons

2 tablespoons dried orange
    peel

6 green cardamom pods,
    gently bruised

1 teaspoon fennel seeds

½ teaspoon dried dandelion
    root

½ teaspoon angelica root

½ teaspoon hyssop

2 cups vodka

1 cup water

2 tablespoons honey

Rhubarb produces a lovely rose-tinged bitters. Make sure you use only the stalks, trimming the ends first, as the leaves are toxic. Use these bitters in any cocktail calling for the ingredient, as well as in the recipe for Strawberry Fields Forever Cocktail (page 139).

Place the rhubarb, lemon zest, orange peel, cardamom, fennel seeds, dandelion root, angelica root, and hyssop in a clean and dry quart-size glass container with an airtight lid (such as a Mason jar). Cover with the vodka and secure the lid tightly. Store the jar in a cool, dark area out of direct sunlight, such as a pantry or bottom cabinet, for 3 weeks. Give the container a shake whenever you think of it.

Strain the liquid through either a fine-mesh strainer, coffee filter, or cheesecloth set over a bowl. Compost the solids. Rinse out the container used for processing, and transfer the infusion into it.

Place the water in a small saucepan. Bring just to boiling. Remove the pan from the heat, add the honey, and whisk to fully combine. Cool to room temperature. Pour the cooled sweetener into the infusion, and secure the lid. Give a shake to combine.

Store the infusion in its infusing location for another 2 days. Using a clean turkey baster, siphon the bitters out of the infusing jar and into a permanent storage container (or into a decorative bottle, if gifting). Take care to avoid any sediment or cloudy matter that may have settled to the bottom. Use within 1 year.

Strawberry Fields Forever Cocktail

Strawberries and rhubarb are often seen together in springtime desserts, so a seasonal cocktail based around the two seemed like a natural fit. To make additional servings, simply multiply the ingredient measurements accordingly.

Place 5 strawberries, heavy cream, vodka, rhubarb bitters, and honey in a blender or food processor. Puree until smooth and creamy. Pour the mixture into a martini glass. Garnish with the remaining frozen strawberry. Serve immediately.

makes 1 serving

6 frozen strawberries, divided

¼ cup + 2 tablespoons heavy
    cream

¼ cup vodka

2 dashes Rhubarb Bitters
    (page 136)

2 teaspoons honey

BITTERS

Composed of roots and spices infused in liquor, culinary bitters are what give certain cocktails their characteristic "oomph." A Manhattan simply wouldn't be what it is without a dash of bitters included. A resurgence of interest in crafting bitters has resulted in a flurry of new domestic purveyors. Not to slight their hard work and skilled, seasoned creations, but why not avoid their sometimes steep costs and make your own? I'm offering four recipes here, each making use of peak-of-ripeness fruits to produce a year's worth of seasonal bitters. Each recipe yields a generous amount of bitters, perfect for gift giving.

Triple Berry Bitters (Summer)

makes 3 cups

1 cup berries (from a combination of blackberries, blueberries, raspberries, etc.)

Zest from 1 lemon

8 whole cloves

One 2-inch cinnamon stick, broken into pieces

1 teaspoon dried rose hips

1 teaspoon dried hibiscus flower

½ teaspoon dried orris root (see Note)

½ teaspoon wild cherry bark

2 cups vodka

1 cup water

2 tablespoons honey

Summer is berry time. Blackberries, blueberries, raspberries, black raspberries, wineberries, mulberries—they're all coming to ripeness in profusion. Tuck them into cobblers, crisps, pies, and jams, but set aside a few cups for bitters, too! Use these bitters in any cocktail calling for the ingredient, as well as in the recipe for the Berry Patch Cocktail (opposite).

Place the berries, lemon zest, cloves, cinnamon, rose hips, hibiscus, orris root, and cherry bark in a clean and dry quart-size glass container with an airtight lid (such as a Mason jar). Cover with the vodka, and secure the lid tightly. Follow the instructions for the Rhubarb Bitters on page 136 to complete the recipe.

Note: Orris root is commonly used in perfumeries for its fragrance, as well as in some types of liquor making, such as many brands of gin. It can be purchased at natural foods stores that have bulk herb sections or online.

The Berry Patch Cocktail

Berries are in abundance come summertime. From raspberries to black-berries covering the color spectrum from golden-hued to wine-stained, berries are quite literally ripe for the picking. This cocktail couples their lovely appearance with their sweet, delicate flavor, resulting in a beautiful and delicious drink showcasing summer's showstoppers.

Begin by straining the berries. Place a fine-mesh sieve over a small bowl. Using the back of a spoon or clean fingers, press on the berries. You want to extract as much juice as possible while leaving the berry's seeds behind in the sieve.

Combine the berry juice, wine, vodka, fruit liqueur, and berry bitters in a glass. Stir gently to combine. Serve with ice.

makes 1 serving

½ cup summer berries, such as raspberries and/or blackberries

¾ cup sparkling rosé wine

2 tablespoons vodka

2 tablespoons fruit liqueur, such as pomegranate or Elderflower Liqueur (page 134)

4 dashes of Triple Berry Bitters (opposite)

Ice, to serve

Pear Bitters (Autumn)

The aroma created by this batch of bitters is simply glorious. Orange peel, pears, and spice render an elixir completely heralding the season at hand. Use these bitters in any cocktail calling for the ingredient, as well as in the recipe for Cozy Cardigan Cocktail (below).

Place the pear pieces, orange zest, dried orange peel, ginger root, allspice, schizandra, calamus, and licorice root in a clean and dry quart-size glass container with an airtight lid (such as a Mason jar). Cover with the vodka, and secure the lid tightly. Follow the instructions for the Rhubarb Bitters on page 136 to complete the recipe, substituting maple syrup for honey.

Note: Schizandra is a woody vine native to Asia. Its berries are used for both culinary and medicinal purposes. Calamus root is quite fragrant and is sometimes used as a substitute for ginger and cinnamon. Both herbs can be found at natural foods stores with bulk herb sections or online.

makes 3 cups

1 cup peeled, cored, and
    chopped pear
Zest from 1 orange
¼ cup dried orange peel
2 teaspoons dried ginger root
1 teaspoon allspice berries
½ teaspoon schizandra ber-
    ries (see Note)
½ teaspoon dried calamus root
    (see Note)
½ teaspoon dried licorice root
    (cut and sifted)
2 cups vodka
1 cup water
2 tablespoons maple syrup

Cozy Cardigan Cocktail

If this drink doesn't put you in an autumnal mood, then I really don't know what will (aside from perhaps a tractor ride through an apple orchard). Apples, pears, cinnamon—the best flavors and scents of the season are all accounted for here.

Fill an 8- to 12-ounce glass with ice. Add the apple juice, pear nectar, pear bitters, and bourbon. Stir to combine. Garnish with the pear wedge and cinnamon stick. Serve immediately.

makes 1 serving

Ice
¼ cup sparkling apple juice
¼ cup + 2 tablespoons Pear
    Nectar (page 30)
3 dashes Pear Bitters (above)
¼ cup bourbon
1 pear wedge
One 2-inch cinnamon stick

Citrus Bitters (Winter)

makes 3 cups

Zest from 4 oranges

1 teaspoon anise seeds

2 star anise

½ teaspoon dried gentian root

½ teaspoon dried burdock root

½ teaspoon juniper berries

½ teaspoon coriander seeds

¼ teaspoon dried sassafras

2 cups vodka

1 cup water

2 tablespoons maple syrup

Any type of oranges will work here. If you can find Seville oranges or blood oranges, they'd be lovely, as well. Use these bitters in any cocktail calling for the ingredient, as well as in the recipe for A Winter's Day Cocktail (opposite).

Place the orange zest, anise seed, star anise, gentian, burdock, juniper, coriander, and sassafras in a clean and dry quart-size glass container with an airtight lid (such as a Mason jar). Cover with the vodka, and secure the lid tightly. Follow the instructions for the Rhubarb Bitters on page 136 to complete the recipe, substituting maple syrup for the honey.

A Winter's Day Cocktail

Gin, citrus bitters, orange juice, and spice combine here to create a delicious homage to the season. Citrus peaks during the winter months, offering a welcome burst of color and flavor.

Fill an 8-ounce glass with ice. Add the gin, orange juice, tonic, bitters, and star anise. Stir to combine. Garnish with a curled orange zest strip and several grates of fresh nutmeg. Serve immediately.

makes 1 serving

Ice

¼ cup + 2 tablespoons gin

Juice from ½ orange

½ cup tonic water

3 dashes Citrus Bitters (opposite)

1 star anise

1 wide strip orange zest, for garnish

Freshly grated nutmeg, for garnish

warming and fermented

The alchemical nature of alcohol has long fascinated me. Mix some sugars with water and yeast, set the concoction aside, and witness an altogether different end product develop. Fermented beverages and hot libations are some of my favorite quenchers. Having a hand in creating them makes the entire process that much more magical.

Earl Grey Hot Toddy

makes 1 serving

1 bag Earl Grey tea

1 cup boiling water

¼ cup whiskey

2 tablespoons fresh lemon juice

Honey, to taste

1 thinly sliced lemon wheel,
    to serve

If you want to step up your hot toddy game, this is the way to go. The citrus from the bergamot in the tea complements the whiskey perfectly. For an additional layer of interest, use one of the flavored whiskeys on pages 115 to 120.

Place the tea bag in a mug. Cover with the boiling water, and steep for 4 minutes. Remove the tea bag without pressing on it. Add the whiskey and lemon juice. Stir gently with a fork to combine. Add honey to taste. Serve with lemon wheel.

GUEST RECIPE | Gin Toddy

makes 1 serving

1 bag ginger tea

1 cup hot water

1 tablespoon honey

2 tablespoons gin

1 lemon slice, to serve

Tracy Benjamin is the kind of friend you want to have. Through her blog Shutterbean, the deft, bold photographer, wife, and mama to Cooper repeatedly shows she's the kind of lady that can pull everything off with aplomb. Whether she's offering gorgeous-sounding (and looking!) skirt steak tacos for Tuesday night's dinner or crafting an enviable cocktail come twilight, she's the go-to gal. We all need a friend who makes life look and sound so effortlessly easy. Here she's sharing her recipe for a gin toddy. I love its twist on the classic cocktail, with the juniper from the gin standing in for whiskey's smoky notes. Add in a bit of ginger tea, some honey, and a lemon slice, and this toddy is downright healthy! You want to be her friend now too, don't you?

Place the tea bag in a mug. Cover with the boiling water, and steep for 4 minutes. Remove the tea bag without pressing on it. Add the honey and gin. Stir well to fully combine. Serve topped with a slice of lemon.

Quenched: Mulled Wine

I held my inaugural Ladies Holiday Cookie Exchange in December 2007. Most of the guests in attendance were coworkers from the doctor's office at which I was then employed. It was very civilized, and gentle, and involved nibbling on a light brunch I'd cooked, followed by exchanging cookies, quiet conversation, and other niceties. Year number two was a bit more rollicking.

Casting my net of invitees a bit wider, I ended up with more than twenty ladies. From the gregarious to the introverted, all personalities were accounted for. Raucous laughter, bawdy talk, and silliness were the order of the day. While it might have been all the sugar we were consuming that attributed to the gaiety and high pitch of the event, it might have just been on account of the wine.

I'd decided to brew up a big batch of mulled wine for my guests. It has been my experience that groups of women, when left with wine, will consume it . . . quickly. I kept this in mind when determining how much to prepare. My hooch, however, was imbibed by my giddy lady friends in no time. We ran out, and in a hurried attempt to warm up a bit more in my Crock-Pot, I added a cool bottle from my basement to the then very hot Crock-Pot. In so doing, I killed my crock. The variation in temperatures caused the crock to crack, effectively ruining my slow cooker and winding down the party.

I've continued hosting my cookie exchange since its debut in 2007. I typically still serve mulled wine at the gathering. Whenever I sip a glass of it now, I'm transported to that Crock-Pot debacle and to all of those wonderful women assembled at that party. Each brought several dozen cookies she'd lovingly baked, a joyful disposition, and a readiness to *get down*. I long ago replaced the Crock-Pot, learning my lesson about temperature fluctuations and hairline fractures in ceramicware. Was I saddened about my ruined Crock-Pot? Sure, but not all that much. Appliances can be replaced, but memories cannot.

Mulled Wine

When the leaves begin to change their hue and the air is continually tinged with the scent of smoke, it's time to put on a pot of mulled wine. This is the recipe I've crafted from years of fireside sipping, and it always pleases.

Combine all of the ingredients except the brandy in a medium-size saucepan or 2-quart Dutch oven. Bring just to the boiling point. Reduce the heat, and simmer for 20 minutes. Remove the pan from the heat. Whisk in the brandy. Serve warm or at room temperature in individual mugs.

makes 5 cups

One 750-ml bottle dry red wine
⅓ cup sugar
Juice and zest from 1 orange
Peel from 1 lemon
2 teaspoons allspice berries
2 teaspoons whole cloves
1 teaspoon black peppercorns
Three 2-inch cinnamon sticks
2 star anise
1½ cups brandy

Glogg

makes 6 cups

Three 2-inch cinnamon sticks

6 green cardamom pods,
     gently bruised

6 whole cloves

One 750-ml bottle dry red
     wine

1 cup Tawny port

1 cup aquavit or vodka

½ cup sugar

Peel from 1 orange

¼ cup raisins

¼ cup slivered or sliced
     almonds

This Swedish spiced wine is the perfect thing to put together when the occasion calls for something a little beyond the usual. Aquavit, a caraway-flavored Swedish liquor, is the traditional addition, but if you can't source it, use vodka.

Place the cinnamon sticks, cardamom pods, and cloves in a small drawstring muslin pouch or twist up in cheesecloth, forming a spice bundle.

In a medium-size saucepan or 2-quart Dutch oven, combine the spice bundle with the wine, port, aquavit or vodka, sugar, and orange peel. Bring to a gentle simmer, stirring until all of the sugar granules are fully dissolved. Remove the pan from the heat. Add in the raisins and almonds. Cover the pot with a lid, and steep for 1 hour. Remove the orange peel and spice bag and compost the solids.

Serve warm in individual cups or mugs, being sure to include a few raisins and almonds in each serving.

How to Make Wine

Brewing wine, mead, and cider at home might seem like a daunting task at first glance. It did to me at least, when I initially looked into it. While different recipes will include slight variations in fermentation time and racking (a term meaning to clarify alcohol, making it clearer once bottled), the steps involved are fairly consistent and straightforward. Sanitizing, fermenting, racking, and bottling are the four stages of creating home-brewed beverages. We'll examine each step here.

Sanitize

Before you begin making wine, mead, or cider, you need to sanitize the equipment you'll be using. This process helps to remove any airborne pathogens that might otherwise compromise the integrity of your homebrew, causing it to spoil. Cleansers specifically intended for wine and beer making can be found at homebrew supply stores, as well as online. My preferred brands are B-Brite, Straight-A, and One Step as they're all nontoxic, my preference for cleaners of all types.

To sanitize, you have two options. You can either place a bit of the sanitizer directly into your fermenting or bottling vessels or dissolve some in warm water and then wash the equipment in the solution, depending on what you're cleaning. Either way, leave the equipment to soak for about ten minutes, and then rinse it in cold water. I've found carboys and bottles easier to sanitize by pouring a bit of the sanitizer into their openings and then filling them with warm water, while airlocks, stoppers, and siphoning tubes work best added to a sink. Follow the instructions on your sanitizer of choice.

Ferment

The next step is the fermentation process itself. As I mentioned, individual recipes will vary in this particular arena. What all will consistently involve, though, is blending fruit with flavorings and yeast, and then leaving the mixture to ferment for various amounts of time. Follow the specifics indicated in the particular recipe you're using.

Rack

Once fermentation ceases, which will be visible by an end to the bubbling that's been going on in your fermentation vessel (usually a 1- or 2-gallon glass jug or carboy), it's time to rack. With your sanitized equipment at the ready, remove the stopper and airlock from the fermentation vessel. Place a siphoning tube (also known as a "racking cane") gently down into the brew. Put this vessel on a counter, chair, or any other location that places it higher than the vessel it will pour into.

Next, place an empty container at a lower level, either on the ground or in a chair. Wherever you put it, bear in mind that it must be lower than the full container, as you'll be using gravity to draw it down. Put the other end of the siphoning tube all of the way into the empty container to minimize the splash and aeration of the brew.

Now it's time to get your brew from its full vessel into the empty one. You can do this one of two ways. If you have an automatic racking cane, which is a device that attaches to the siphoning tube, simply pull it up and down to siphon the liquid into the empty container. Otherwise, using your mouth, gently suck on the lower end of the siphoning tube (the higher end should be in the brew), until the liquid begins traveling out of the full vessel. Lower the tube into the empty container and allow the liquid to move down.

When the brew is just about fully transitioned over and you're down near the bottom of the formerly full vessel (the murky portion remaining is known as the "lees"), stop siphoning. If your recipe indicates or your preference dictates a need to ferment further (to allow the flavor to develop, let the brew clear, or to increase the alcohol content), place a sanitized stopper into the neck of the newly filled jug. Discard the lees. Otherwise, it's time to bottle!

Bottle

Transferring your homebrew from its fermentation and racking vessels to individual bottles is the last step. If your brew had extra fermentation time, follow the steps above for racking before bottling. If you racked and didn't give your brew additional time in the fermentation bottle, simply pour the liquid into individual bottles using a funnel. Alternatively, plastic food-grade buckets with dispensers are very handy.

When selecting bottles, you can use standard wine or beer bottles, capping them with corks or caps. Swing- or flip-top-style bottles are another bottling option. You can purchase any of these bottles new, either from homebrew supply stores or online, or repurpose bottles that previously housed commercially prepared beverages.

GUEST RECIPE | Dandelion and Honeysuckle Wine

makes 1½ to 2 gallons

2½ quarts dandelion flowers (see Note)

2 quarts honeysuckle flowers (see Note)

7 quarts boiling water

4 to 6 pounds sugar (see Note)

Juice, peels, and pulp from 2 lemons (avoid any white pith from the peels)

Juice, peels, and pulp from 2 oranges (avoid any white pith from the peels)

½ packet champagne yeast (see Note)

¼ teaspoon yeast nutrient (see Note)

2 cups golden raisins, dried figs, or dried apricots (optional, for additional flavor)

EQUIPMENT

2-gallon fermentation vessel. Make sure all equipment is sanitized before use. See page 155 for sanitizing instructions.

I first met Heather Grissom at my house. Which is to say, I'd opened my home to teach a canning class, and she was one of the attendees. We've remained in touch ever since. Heather works by day on her family's small farm in Durham, North Carolina, and by night as a doula. She's also deeply enamored of all things homesteading and shares them on her blog Lettuce Turnip the Beet. *As she describes it, "From growing and raising to harvesting and preserving, I enjoy it all and try to encourage others to become involved in keeping up this wonderful tradition." Here she's sharing her recipe for Dandelion and Honeysuckle Wine, a glorious use of summer's wildflowers if there ever was one.*

Place the dandelion and honeysuckle flowers in a large glass or ceramic container for soaking, such as a crock. Pour the boiling water over the flowers, cover with a dish towel secured by a rubber band, and carefully place a lid over the container. Let it stand in a warm place for 2 days and no longer, stirring a couple times a day.

Pour the flower and water mixture into a large pot and bring to a low boil. Add the sugar and citrus peels, and stir. Keep on a low boil for 1 hour, then cover and allow the mixture to cool. Now add the pulp and juice, stir, and transfer the mixture into another crock/container for fermentation. Stir in the champagne yeast and yeast nutrient. Cover and let sit in a warm place for 3 days, stirring daily.

Strain the liquid through a fine-mesh sieve or cheesecloth, squeezing out as much liquid as possible. Compost the solids. Transfer the liquid into a secondary fermentation vessel (I use plastic ones fashioned from tubs from a local brew supply store; however, you could easily make your own or use a crock made for fermenting). If adding extra fruit for flavor, add it now; please note, however, the darker color of some fruits will change the color of the wine (I prefer golden raisins or figs for their light color).

Cover with a lid, and allow the mixture to proceed until fermentation has stopped—this will be visible by a cessation of bubbling. (At this point, you could attach a fermentation trap to the container to help monitor fermentation. You can also use a hydrometer to track the progress of your wine; take your first measurement at around day 7 to 10, and then measure every day thereafter. I aim for a hydrometer reading anywhere from 1.08 for a sweeter wine to 1.002 for a drier wine, with my preference at 1.04.) Fermentation will occur quickly at first and then slow down. I usually rack the wine at around 3 weeks; this seems to be a good reference point with flower wines.

When you are ready to rack the wine, siphon the liquid into a sanitized container (you'll rack the wine one more time, so you can use any container at this point). See page 156 for racking instructions. If you used extra fruit in the second fermentation, strain the liquid through cheesecloth, squeezing the cloth to remove any remaining liquid. Compost the solids. Secure the container, and set aside again for 3 months. Store in a cool, dark spot, such as a basement or pantry.

Rack a final time, this time transferring the wine into individual bottles. See page 156 for bottling instructions. I prefer to use glass bottles with locking lids or bottles with caps due to the sparkling quality of this wine. As with all dandelion wines, let it sit in the bottle in a cool, dark place for at least 6 months; however, 1 year is much preferred. Enjoy on a hot summer day chilled, over ice with some fresh herbs.

Note: Pick the dandelion and honeysuckle flowers when open, mid-morning to early afternoon, and use immediately. Rinse and remove the flowers from their stalks and any other green matter, leaving only the petals. This process is time-consuming but helps to remove any bitter flavors that might otherwise get imparted.

The amount of sugar used is up to you. Use more if you want a sweeter wine, less for one more mild.

Champagne yeast and yeast nutrient both can be sourced from homebrew supply stores and online.

GUEST RECIPE | Rose Wine

makes 1 gallon

¾ gallon water

1¼ cups dried rose petals, crumbled (double amount if using fresh petals)

1 cup dried chamomile

½ cup dried hibiscus flowers

1 inch fresh ginger, chopped

5 to 10 pieces of dried fruit (such as cherries, raisins, apples, or other fruit)

1 slice dried lemon

2 cups sugar

½ packet Montrechet champagne yeast (see Note)

Simple syrup (optional, recipe follows)

1 drop rose water (optional)

FOR THE SIMPLE SYRUP

1 cup water

2 cups sugar or 1½ cups honey or agave nectar

EQUIPMENT

1-gallon glass jug, rubber stopper, airlock, siphoning tube, fine-mesh sieve, and a funnel. Make sure all equipment is sanitized before use. See page 155 for sanitizing instructions.

Amber Shehan knows a thing or two (or fifty) about herbs. As it turns out, she also lives just down the road from me, calling the same small western North Carolina town home. Her love of all things herbal often gets bottled up and fermented, as is the case with the recipe for a glorious Rose Wine she's sharing here. She blogs at Swamp Pixie Herbal, *where she posts her thoughts and rambles about herbalism, gardening, recipes, brewing, backyard chickens, canning, book reviews, and other such goodness.*

Bring the water to a boil in a medium-size saucepan. Remove from the heat. Add the remaining ingredients except the yeast, simple syrup, and rose water. Stir to mix, and cover with a lid. Steep for 15 to 30 minutes.

Put the funnel in the neck of the gallon jug, and place the sieve on the funnel. Strain the warm liquid through the fine-mesh sieve into the gallon jug. Compost the solids. Add cold water to bring the liquid level to the neck of the jug. Attach the rubber stopper and airlock to the jug, and let it cool.

Once the glass jug has cooled to body temperature, sprinkle in the yeast. The yeast will begin to dissolve and settle, and you can gently swish the liquid around to speed that process up a bit. Wrap the jug in a cloth to protect it from light, and store it in a clean, dark place until it has completed fermentation. You will know when it is done fermenting when there are no more bubbles and the body clears. This can take anywhere from 1 month to 6 weeks, sometimes longer depending on the sugar content.

At this point before racking and bottling, you may want to taste the wine (I do this by sanitizing a drinking straw and taking a tiny taste straight from the jug). If it isn't sweet enough, you can add the simple syrup. To make the simple syrup, bring the water to a boil. Add the sugar, and stir until dissolved. Let it cool before adding to the wine. If it isn't floral enough, you can add just a drop of rose water to encourage the floral notes.

See page 156 for racking and bottling instructions.

Note: Montrechet champagne yeast is available at homebrew supply stores and online. Store any unused portion in a sealed container in the refrigerator, and use within 1 week.

GUEST RECIPE | Hedgerow Wine

makes 1 gallon

¾ gallon water

5 to 10 pieces of dried fruit (such as cherries, raisins, or apples)

1 slice dried lemon

¼ cup dried elderflower blossoms or 2 cups fresh

2 cups sugar

2 to 3 cups packed fresh honeysuckle flowers, green bits removed

¼ cup fresh yarrow flowers

¼ cup fresh red clover flower heads

½ packet Montrechet champagne yeast (see Note)

Simple syrup (recipe follows)

FOR THE *SIMPLE SYRUP*

1 cup water

2 cups sugar or 1½ cups honey or agave nectar

EQUIPMENT

Bucket, 1-gallon glass jug, rubber stopper, airlock, siphoning tube, fine-mesh sieve, and a funnel. Make sure all equipment is sanitized before use. See page 155 for sanitizing instructions.

Here's another recipe generously provided by Amber Shehan. Along with her Rose Wine (page 162), she's offering tips for transforming elderflower, honeysuckle, yarrow, and red clover flowers into a fragrant, floral wine.

Bring the water to a boil in a medium-size saucepan. Add the dried fruit and dried elderflowers. Stir to combine. Remove the pan from the heat. Add the sugar, and stir until the granules have fully dissolved.

Place the prepared, fresh flowers into a sanitized bucket (or large stock pot), and pour the hot dried fruit and flower mixture on top. Stir to mix, cover with a lid or plate, and leave to steep. Allow the mixture to cool about 1 hour.

Put the funnel in the neck of the gallon jug, and place the sieve on the funnel. Strain the liquid through the fine-mesh sieve into the gallon jug. Add cold water to bring the liquid level with the neck of the jug. Attach the rubber stopper and airlock to the jug, and let it cool.

Once the glass jug has cooled to body temperature, sprinkle in the yeast. The yeast will begin to dissolve and settle, and you can gently swish the liquid around to speed that process up a bit. Wrap the jug in a cloth to protect it from light, and store it in a clean, dark place until it has completed fermentation. You will know when it is done fermenting when there are no more bubbles and the body clears. This can take anywhere from 1 month to 6 weeks, sometimes longer depending on the sugar content.

At this point before bottling, you may want to taste the wine (I do this by sanitizing a drinking straw and taking a tiny taste straight from the jug). If it isn't sweet enough, you can add the simple syrup. To make the simple syrup, bring the water to a boil. Add the sugar, and stir until dissolved. Let it cool before adding to the wine.

Now it's time to rack. See page 156 for racking and bottling instructions.

Note: Montrechet champagne yeast is available at homebrew supply stores and online. Store any unused portion in a sealed container in the refrigerator, and use within 1 week.

GUEST RECIPE | Walnut Wine (Vin de Noix)

makes six 750-ml bottles

---

40 fresh walnuts (see Note)

1 gallon inexpensive red wine (a medium-bodied varietal, such as Shiraz, Pinot Noir, or even Rosé)

Citrus and spices from list below (optional)

3 cups sugar

One 750-ml bottle vodka

Optional Flavorings

1 to 2 tablespoons orange and lemon zest

1 teaspoon ground cinnamon

½ teaspoon ground cloves

½ teaspoon ground nutmeg

Equipment

2-gallon crock, sieve, corks, funnel, six 750-ml wine bottles. Make sure all equipment is sanitized before use. See page 155 for sanitizing instructions.

It was goats that first brought Thomas Yeska and me together. The self-described "spiritual seeker, life lover, joy spreader, musician, homesteader, plant aficionado, and student of self-sufficiency" was, like myself, considering bringing a goat or two into his life and onto his land. A mutual goat-owning friend had invited us both to her property to see what such an endeavor involved. While neither of us ended up pursuing that consideration, we did forge a friendship in the process, discovering we shared interests in more than just milk-producing mammals. Thomas is offering here his recipe for Walnut Wine that he learned while living in France. Possessed of an "unquenchable thirst for travel and adventure," he's traversed the globe, learning about agricultural, botanical, and culinary practices worldwide. His wanderlust is now our delicious beverage!

Begin by prepping the walnuts. Fresh walnuts will have an outer green shell, which you'll cut and use alongside the inner meat. Cut each nut into quarters, saving all of the clear juices they dispense. This can best be done by cutting them on a plastic cutting board with a rim or lip for holding in liquid. Place the walnuts and wine into a 2-gallon crock. If using citrus or spices, add them now. Cover with a bit of cheesecloth and store at room temperature for 6 weeks.

Strain the wine through a fine-mesh sieve placed atop a large bowl. It will now be a very dark color and stain easily, so be mindful of your clothing or other items that could be darkened while straining. Compost the solids. Add the sugar and vodka to the wine. Stir well to dissolve the sugar granules.

Using a funnel, bottle the wine, dividing it evenly among 6 sanitized wine bottles. There may be a bit of must or residue in the liquid, but that's alright. No need to rack it. Cork the bottles, and leave to age at least 4 months.

Note: Quarter the nuts with a large knife or cleaver. The walnuts are still green and somewhat soft at this point. There really isn't a well-formed hull or nut at this stage. It works with all walnuts harvested when about the size of a golf ball, including black walnuts, English walnuts, and other varieties.

GUEST RECIPE | Wineberry Wine

Along with his recipe for Walnut Wine (opposite), Thomas Yeska is also sharing a recipe for creating a berry-based wine. Wineberry is a species of raspberry native to China, Japan, and Korea originally brought to Europe and North America as an ornamental. Its flavor is a cross between the sweetness of a raspberry and the puckeryness of a sour cherry or cranberry. If you can't find wineberries, wild raspberries or blackberries may be used instead.

Bring the water to a boil in a large saucepan or stock pot. Add the sugar, and stir until the granules have fully dissolved. Transfer the mixture to a large nonmetallic (plastic, glass, or ceramic) food-grade container (it will need to have a capacity larger than 1 gallon, as you'll be adding that much liquid plus additional ingredients). Add the berries, mashing them slightly with a hand blender or potato masher. Add the cinnamon and mint. When the mixture is lukewarm, stir in the yeast. Cover the container with a nonairtight cover, such as cheesecloth or a kitchen towel. Allow the mixture to ferment for 7 to 10 days at room temperature, stirring it twice a day.

Strain the mixture through cheesecloth. Compost the solids. Transfer the liquid to a 1-gallon carboy or glass jug. Seal with the rubber stopper and airlock. Set aside at room temperature to ferment.

When the bubbling stops and fermentation ends 1 to 2 weeks later (the warmer the fermentation location, the faster fermentation will occur), leave it to age in a cool, dark location, such as a basement, crawlspace, kitchen pantry, or bottom cabinet, for 6 weeks to 6 months (once this second fermentation stops bubbling, as long as you have an airlock in your bottle, it doesn't really matter when you bottle it, as long as it's done within 6 months).

Siphon the wine to get rid of the sediment, if desired, and bottle. See page 156 for racking and bottling instructions. Alternatively, place a stopper in the jug and leave unfiltered.

makes 1 gallon

1 gallon water

6 cups sugar

6 cups wineberries, other wild raspberries, or blackberries

3 cinnamon sticks

2 tablespoons chopped fresh spearmint or other mint leaves

½ teaspoon champagne yeast or other wine yeast

EQUIPMENT

Large food-grade container, 1-gallon glass jug or carboy, rubber stopper, airlock, siphoning tube. Make sure all equipment is sanitized before use. See page 155 for sanitizing instructions.

makes 5 gallons

5 pounds raspberries

4 pounds elderberries

1 gallon + ¾ cup honey,
    divided

1 gallon + 2 cups water,
    divided + extra water to fill
    your carboy

1 whole nutmeg, grated

1 packet Lavlin 1CV-D47
    yeast (see Note)

EQUIPMENT

Two 5-gallon carboys, rubber
    stopper, airlock, siphon-
    ing tube. Make sure all
    equipment is sanitized
    before use. See page 155
    for sanitizing instructions.

GUEST RECIPE | # Raspberry and Elderberry Melomel

It's great, when you have a little one in your life, to have a friend you can turn to for professional medical advice. That's the case for me with my friend Maria Muscarella. Maria and I met in high school when she was a senior and I was a sophomore. A registered nurse as well as an herbalist, Maria is my go-to gal whenever my son has something going on medically that I'm not sure warrants a visit to the doctor proper. As well as a gifted healer, she's also an enormously talented crafter, seamstress, knitter, aerial silks acrobat, gardener, cook, chicken mama, beekeeper, home-schooling mama to Kaia and Leif, and wife to Toby. Here she's sharing her recipe for Raspberry and Elderberry Melomel, the term used to describe meads made from honey and fruit. You can keep up with Maria and her family on her blog Dirt Under My Nails.

Place your berries (in batches if needed) in a blender and mash them up. Strain through fine cheesecloth, squeezing out and reserving the berry juice and composting the seeds.

Pour all of the berry juice into a 5-gallon carboy. The carboy will be hard to move when it's full, so make sure it's in a good spot that is out of direct sunlight before beginning to fill it up.

In a large stock pot (big enough to hold at least 2½ gallons), warm 1 gallon of the honey and 1 gallon of the water over medium-low heat while stirring gently to dilute the honey (you don't want this to simmer or boil; simply mix the honey and water together to combine). Let this cool to 90°F. Add the grated nutmeg and the yeast, and stir to incorporate. Pour this into your carboy with your juice. Then add enough water (at about 90°F) to fill the carboy to the 5-gallon mark.

Affix an airlock and wrap the carboy in a blanket or towels, leaving the airlock peeking out of the top. Within a day or two, you should begin to see bubbles popping up in the airlock. This will continue for a few weeks. When it has slowed to one bubble every few minutes or has completely stopped, it's time to rack it.

Just before racking, place 2 cups of water and ¾ cup of honey into a pot, and warm on the stove to mix well. Let it cool. Pour it into a fresh carboy that will be used for racking.

Rack the melomel into the carboy that has your honey water, leaving the spent yeast in the bottom of the old carboy. The honey water will give the yeast a little food to create a bit more carbonation in your bottles. See page 156 for racking instructions.

From here, you can replace the airlock and let the mead settle again, racking it a second time for even more clarity, or you can bottle it up See page 156 for bottling instructions. You can drink your mead right away, but the flavor will be much better if you let it age at least 6 months.

Note: Lavlin 1CV-D 47 yeast is available at homebrew supply stores and online.

makes 4 gallons (sixteen 750-ml bottles)

---

4 gallons spring water

1 gallon local honey

Additional flavorings from list below (optional, choose one)

10 drops vanilla extract per jug
(optional)

OPTIONAL FLAVORINGS

Seasonal fruit, such as wild
blueberries, apples and
pears, or tomatoes

Burdock, chicory, and dandelion root

Dried herbs (lavender is a
favorite)

Dried spices such as ginger,
cardamom, cloves, pepper,
cinnamon, and star anise

Coffee (substitute brewed
coffee for equal parts water)

EQUIPMENT

Two 5-gallon buckets, long
spoon, kitchen cloth, 4 clean
1-gallon glass jugs, rubber
stoppers, airlocks, fine-mesh
sieve, funnel, 16 clean wine
bottles (recycled or new),
corks, and corker. Make sure
all equipment is sanitized
before use. See page 155 for
sanitizing instructions.

GUEST RECIPE | Janell's Alche'mead

Janell Kapoor is a Renaissance woman for the new age. The Ashevillage Institute and Kleiwerks International founder has created an urban educational center in Asheville, North Carolina, where she and a variety of educators teach and showcase the core beliefs and techniques of the agricultural system known as permaculture. While visits to Ashevillage are always inspirational, during a recent visit I saw bottle upon bottle of mead bubbling away in the dining room. She's graciously sharing a recipe for one of her many mead concoctions here.

Start by deciding if you want to make a plain mead or a mead with added ingredients. If you plan to add flavors, start by preparing your ingredients. If using dried herbs or roots, make them into a strong tea or decoction, then strain and compost the solids. Substitute the tea/decoction for an equal amount of water. If using fresh fruits, chop them finely or mash them. Add your tea, decoction, or fruit to the bucket.

Add the water and honey to the bucket. You can swish some of the water in the honey jar and shake it with the lid on to get all excess honey out.

If you added fresh fruit to the bucket, add as much water as you need to fill the bucket, while leaving enough room to stir. Stir and cover with a cloth. Stir 3 to 5 times a day for approximately 1 week, or until it foams a bit while you stir.

After about 1 week (give or take a couple days), your mead should be foamy when you stir it. This is a sign of fermentation. Strain the mead through a fine-mesh sieve placed over another bucket. Compost the solids. Funnel this strained liquid into clean, 1-gallon jugs, and attach airlocks to them. Label each bottle with the ingredients and date. Keep in a semiwarm space, out of direct sunlight.

After 3 to 6 months, bubbling in the airlock will cease. At this point, wrap your jugs in a towel, and set them in a hot and sunny spot. If they do not bubble anymore, all the sugars have been digested and/or the yeast is dead; your mead is ready to bottle.

Strain the mead through a fine-mesh sieve set atop a large bowl, pot, or pitcher. When you get toward the bottom of the jug, when the liquid starts to get cloudy, stop pouring. That's the dead yeast, which has a distinct flavor that I give to my compost.

Now, taste the mead. Do you like it? Pour a small amount into a shot glass and add a tiny drop of vanilla extract. Do you like that flavor more? If so, add a few drops into each bottle. If you add too much sweetness, it could reactivate the yeast and your bottle could explode, so use the vanilla sparingly! Funnel the mead into your clean wine bottles. See page 156 for bottling instructions. Then cork the tops and label each bottle. Voilà, you're done!

When serving, I like to chill my mead in case the yeast got reactivated. By chilling before opening the bottle, the yeast will go dormant, and your bottle won't explode when you open it.

GUEST RECIPE | Wassail

*makes 10 to
11 cups*

½ gallon fresh apple cider

1 cup orange juice

1 cup unsweetened cranberry
    juice

½ cup honey

6 to 8 cinnamon sticks

Whole cloves (a handful)

Several chunks of fresh ginger

Rum, to taste (optional)

Wassail covers many bases. It is at once a wish for good health, a hot bever-age, and a traditional British ceremony that blesses apple trees for a fruitful harvest the following year. This recipe comes from Byron Ballard, a writer, scholar, and expert on nature-based traditions and folklore. Don't forget to wassail your trees, per her suggestion, by offering them the very first cup!

Combine all of the ingredients except the rum in a deep pot or Dutch oven. Whisk gently to combine. Simmer the mixture over the lowest setting at least 3 hours, stirring periodically. When you feel the flavors have all come together to your liking, remove the pot from the heat. If desired, stir in the rum in an amount to your inclination and taste pref-erence. Serve warm. Store any unused portion in the refrigerator, and use within 1 to 2 weeks.

GUEST RECIPE | Hard Cider

Trevor Baker and I go way back. We met our first year of college and were inseparable for the next two. Time has brought both of us away from and later back to Asheville, North Carolina. Trevor's mother is British, and trips across the pond in his youth set the stage for a lifetime love affair with hard cider. Recently, he took his passion full-time, creating Asheville's first locally sourced and bottled offering, Noble Cider. He's sharing here his go-to recipe for a home batch of cider. When apple season rolls around, I know what he'll be doing, and I highly encourage you to do the same!

final amount depends on how many times you rack your cider. expect to lose 1 or 2 cups per racking

---

1 gallon apple juice (see Note)
Several tablespoons sugar
1 package champagne yeast
    and yeast nutrient (see
    Note)

Equipment

Hydrometer, hydrometer
    test jar, thermometer,
    airlock, rubber stopper,
    rubber stopper without
    hole, two 1-gallon carboys,
    siphoning tube. Make sure
    all equipment is sanitized
    before use. See page 155
    for sanitizing instructions.

Test the sugar level of the fresh juice by pouring a sample of the juice into the test jar. Drop in the hydrometer. The temperature of the juice makes a difference in gravity reading, so get the juice close to 60°F before testing it. There are usually two or three different measuring scales on a hydrometer. I personally like to use specific gravity. If your gravity is below 1.040 (about 5% alcohol by volume, or ABV), consider adding sugar to avoid potential microbial problems in your finished hard cider. The more sugar you add, the higher your alcohol level. Place the juice into the sanitized carboy.

Rehydrate the yeast by following the instructions on the package closely. You will need a basic household thermometer. Add the yeast slurry to the juice, and mix it well. Add some yeast nutrients per the instructions on the package. I would err on the side of adding a tad extra, since apple juice is typically low in nitrogen. Mix it up well.

Attach the airlock/stopper combo to the carboy, being sure to fill it with water. It helps to dry the inside of the lid area and the outside of the stopper to ensure a good tight seal. Place the carboy in a quiet corner or basement, and let the yeast work its magic.

Agitate the liquid every day, until the end of fermentation. Just swirl it around for ½ minute, making sure the bottom sediment gets moved about. This keeps all the yeast happy—you don't want any living yeast to get trapped under a blanket of sediment or they start stressing out!

Depending on various factors, the fermentation process can range from 1 week to a few months. Once the bubbles stop, you should start testing the gravity every couple of days. Let it ferment to "dry," no sugar left. Basically, a 1.000 (or slightly lower) specific gravity means that the yeast has eaten all the sugar.

Once it's done, take off the airlock/stopper combo. Replace with a clean and sanitized solid stopper. Place the bottle in the refrigerator for 1 to 2 days to help the sediment/yeast settle to the bottom. Take it out, and siphon into the other clean, sanitized carboy. See page 156 for racking instructions. Try not to suck up too much sediment as you rack the cider. The goal is to leave behind as much sediment as possible. Multiple rackings are fine; just let the cider settle before siphoning again.

Top off the carboy with the siphoned cider with clean water or left-over "dry" cider from a previous batch to just below the neck. Topping off helps keep oxygen out of the carboy. Let the cider mature in a cool/cold environment, below 60°F, for 1 to 2 months (if you can resist not drinking it all straight away!). If you used true cider apples, leave it to mature for a longer period of time. Maturing the cider will allow the flavors to mellow and the sulfur smell from the yeast to dissipate.

Avoid getting too much oxygen exposure to the finished cider; to do so, transfer the cider to smaller containers as you drink it and keep it in the fridge. If you like a sweeter hard cider, then simply add sweetener to individual servings. Experiment with different sweeteners and varying intensity.

Note: Ideally, you have access to a cider apple tree, an apple grinder, and a press to make juice. Most of us don't. The next best thing is fresh, un-pasteurized, no-preservatives-added juice from a local orchard. You can use juice from a store, or even juice concentrate. Avoid juice with lots of potassium sorbate, as it will inhibit yeast growth. If you have your own tree and equipment, 1 bushel yields about 3 gallons of juice. Apple varieties vary from region to region, so ask around to find out what's available. Here in North Carolina, I like to use Stayman Winesap, Mutsu, Arkansas Black, Pink Lady, Jonathan, Granny Smith, Cortland, and Goldrush. Blending varieties usually makes the best cider. Experiment with crab apples and wild apples, too.

It's fun to experiment with different yeasts, so try out a few. American and European ale yeasts are quite nice and add new flavor profiles to hard cider. Pick a yeast that can tolerate the normal temperature range in your house, barn, or wherever you choose to allow the cider to ferment. If you live in a hot climate without air-conditioning, don't buy yeast that stresses out over 65°F.

Quenched: Hard Cider

Several weeks after my thirtieth birthday, I took myself and a friend to the United Kingdom. I'd never been anywhere in Europe at that point, and was ready to transform my armchair musings into lived experiences. Not letting lack of funds stand in my way, I applied for a credit card with a modest credit line, received it, and began planning my travel itinerary.

The early August afternoon that we flew out of Atlanta Hartsfield Airport, it was 104°F. My overnight attire, accordingly, consisted of sandals and a thin sundress. A last-minute flight change at the airport, which also involved a change of airline, resulted in our luggage being lost once arriving the next morning at Heathrow Airport in London. Our suitcases would remain lost for the next forty-five days!

Arriving as I had in only a gauzy sundress and flimsy shoes, my plans to travel to the Highlands of western Scotland a few days later necessitated some shopping. Having to purchase a travel wardrobe might sound like a wonderful problem to have, but that couldn't have been further from the truth. Having to allocate my limited funds toward clothing purchases meant scrimping elsewhere.

What resulted was some paltry meals and clothing purchased at inexpensive retail stores. Where I didn't scrimp, however, was on hard cider. Drinking pints of hard cider, one of my most beloved beverages, while in the United Kingdom was one of my no-compromise vows. To sit in a pub (or, well, many) and knock back a pint (or two) was required travel activity, I pledged.

The highlight of the trip came toward its conclusion. The day before we were to head home, my friend and I took a ferry out to the tiny isle of Eigg, Scotland. Incredibly, though there was very little in the way of human activity to be witnessed (and where the sheep clearly, considerably outnumbered the human residents), the island was in the possession of a quaint café. More important, that quaint café had pints of hard cider on tap.

My friend and I took our beverages to an outdoor picnic table. There we sat, watching the tide come in to the accompaniment of a bagpipe player in the background (I kid you not). While my plans hadn't unfolded quite in the way I'd imagined, I was having the time of my life. I quenched my travel-weary thirst, shared a contented sigh with my traveling companion, and thanked my lucky stars for having the courage and gumption to take myself just where I wanted to go.

festive

From punches to pitchers, these beverages are, quite often, the life of the party. Or perhaps, at the very least, the liquid life! They're the libations that set the mood and characterize the flavor of celebrations and festive occasions. A number of them taste even better if given a bit of infusing time, so do be sure to plan ahead.

Eggnog

6 large eggs

2 cups whole milk

2 cups heavy cream, divided

½ cup sugar

2 teaspoons vanilla extract

½ cup bourbon

½ cup dark rum or brandy

Freshly grated nutmeg, to
    serve

Even before Thanksgiving Day appears on the calendar, it's likely I've already downed a mug or two of eggnog. I just can't get enough of the creamy, rich beverage. To me, it's the unofficial signal that the holiday season has arrived. If you'd like to serve this to underage drinkers, omit the alcohol and increase both the milk and cream by half a cup.

Begin by prepping an ice bath. Fill a sink ¾ full with cold water and ice cubes. Whisk the eggs. Place the eggs, milk, 1 cup of heavy cream, and sugar in a medium-size saucepan. Cook over medium heat until the custard easily coats the back of a spoon and has thickened slightly. Remove the pan from the heat, and place the bottom directly into the prepared ice bath. Whisk in the vanilla and continue to whisk for 3 to 4 minutes, until the ingredients are fully combined. Transfer the saucepan to a kitchen counter. Cover with a lid, and allow to cool until near room temperature, about 1 hour.

Strain the egg mixture through a fine-mesh sieve set atop a bowl. Discard any egg solids caught in the sieve. Whisk the bourbon and rum or brandy into the egg custard. In a separate bowl, beat the remaining 1 cup of heavy cream until light and billowy. Gently fold the whipped cream into the egg custard. Transfer to the refrigerator. Chill overnight or at least 4 hours.

Serve either in individual glasses or in a small bowl with a ladle. Grate fresh nutmeg liberally over the top just before serving.

Spring Sangria

makes 4 to 5 cups

One 750-ml bottle white wine

¼ cup + 2 tablespoons brandy

2 pints strawberries, hulled
    and chopped

¼ cup pomegranate liquor
    (see Note)

3 tablespoons sugar

Ice, to serve

Strawberries are the star in this sangria. Choose a crisp white wine such as Pinot Grigio or Sauvignon Blanc. This sangria would be lovely to serve at a Mother's Day brunch, wedding showers (for all those June brides!), or college graduation parties.

Combine all of the ingredients in a large glass bowl or container (such as a ½-gallon Mason jar or canister). Stir with a wooden spoon to help dissolve the sugar granules. Cover with a lid, place in the refrigerator, and steep at least 4 hours, longer if possible. The longer the wine steeps, the more intense the flavors become.

Serve in individual glasses with ice. Store any unused portion in the refrigerator. Use within 1 week.

Note: If pomegranate liquor is not available, substitute an equal amount of juice.

SANGRIA

A Spanish beverage composed of red or white wine, fresh fruit, fruit juice, sugar, and, often, sparkling water and brandy, sangria is one of my most beloved beverages for a crowd. It's always well received and can be affordable and easy to make. Too often, though, folks forget about sangria and its profound deliciousness outside of summer. Here I'm offering a year's worth of seasonal sangria recipes. Capitalizing on the fruits at their peak of seasonal ripeness, my sangrias will have you and your guests uttering *Muy bueno!* with each sip.

Summer Sangria

In my mind, summertime is all about stone fruits. Here peaches are blended with an apricot, a plum, and a nectarine, creating a sangria that's as lovely to look at as it is to sip.

Combine all of the ingredients in a large glass bowl or container (such as a ½-gallon Mason jar or canister). Stir with a wooden spoon to help dissolve the sugar granules. Cover with a lid, place in the refrigerator, and steep for at least 4 hours, longer if possible. The longer the wine steeps, the more intense the flavors become.

Serve in individual glasses with ice. Store any unused portion in the refrigerator. Use within 1 week.

makes 4 to 5 cups

One 750-ml bottle white wine
¼ cup + 2 tablespoons brandy
¼ cup orange liqueur
2 peaches, pitted and sliced
1 apricot, pitted and sliced
1 plum, pitted and sliced
1 nectarine, pitted and sliced
2 tablespoons sugar
Ice, to serve

Autumn Sangria

A bit of gin is the unexpected element in this sangria. The juniper flavor it imparts, along with several of the berries themselves, gives the sangria an overarching freshness. Select pears that offer a slight yield when gently pressed, indicating ripeness.

Combine all of the ingredients in a large glass bowl or container (such as a ½-gallon Mason jar or canister). Stir with a wooden spoon to fully combine. Cover with a lid, place in the refrigerator, and steep for at least 4 hours, longer if possible. The longer the wine steeps, the more intense the flavors become.

Serve in individual glasses with ice. Store any unused portion in the refrigerator. Use within 1 week.

Note: If apple brandy is not available, substitute an equal amount of regular brandy.

makes 4 to 5 cups

One 750-ml bottle Rioja
¼ cup + 2 tablespoons apple
    brandy (see Note)
3 tablespoons gin
1 apple, cored and thinly
    sliced
2 pears, cored and thinly
    sliced
1 cup Pear Nectar (page 30)
6 juniper berries
6 whole cloves
One 2-inch cinnamon stick
Ice, to serve

Winter Sangria

makes 4 to 5 cups

One 750-ml bottle Rioja
1 cup fresh orange juice
1 lemon, thinly sliced
1 lime, thinly sliced
1 orange, thinly sliced
2 tablespoons sugar
One 2-inch cinnamon stick
1 star anise
¼ cup + 2 tablespoons brandy
¼ cup orange liqueur
Ice, to serve

Citrus is at its peak of ripeness come winter. That translates to sweet, juicy fruits just begging to be added to a pitcher of sangria. Here I've included a bit of cinnamon and star anise for some spice undertones. This sangria would be a lovely complement to a warming pork roast or roasted chicken on a frosty winter's evening.

Combine all of the ingredients in a large glass bowl or container (such as a ½-gallon Mason jar or canister). Stir with a wooden spoon to help dissolve the sugar granules. Cover with a lid, place in the refrigerator, and steep for at least 4 hours, longer if possible. The longer the wine steeps, the more intense the flavors become.

Serve in individual glasses with ice. Store any unused portion in the refrigerator. Use within 1 week.

Quenched: Sangria

I am not the sort of lady who likes to date. I never have. That whole flirty, coquettish thing just never really worked for me. I'm far too much of a heart-on-my-sleeve, all-cards-on-the-table person to ever be coy. I can barely keep birthday or holiday gifts a secret from their intended recipient, so holding my feelings at bay for a person of affection just doesn't come naturally to me. I had just a handful of boyfriends as a youth and four more before I met the man I'd marry. Fortunately for me, he operated under the same set of dating guidelines.

Our very first date, which occurred four days after a mutual friend introduced us online, took place January 1, 2007. We met for dinner at a Salvadoran restaurant in Asheville, North Carolina, Tomato Cocina Latina. Possessed of a deep, gravelly voice on the phone and a large barrel chest in some online photos I saw, I wasn't quite sure what to expect from this man who seemed too good to be true. I was already quite smitten with him from our digital and phone interactions, so I was curious to see if any chemistry would evidence itself when we sat face to face.

I arrived first, and I remember thinking as I watched him walk up to the restaurant that I intended to put no expectations on our meeting. As he approached my table, I sensed a gentle energy despite his stature. We hugged, he removed his coat, and we ordered a pitcher of sangria. Over the next two hours, I enjoyed one of the best meals of my life, both culinarily and romantically. This man, I told myself, was a keeper. Clearly reciprocating the emotion I felt, as we slowly descended the restaurant's front steps, he told me he'd see me again as soon as I wanted to see him. That proved to be the next evening, and the one thereafter, and pretty much every night since.

Two weeks after our inaugural date, Glenn proposed marriage. I accepted, and we married four and a half months later in the field just down the hill from our little house up on a mountain knob. Whenever I sip a glass of sangria now, I think of that fateful encounter and how sometimes you just know when you've found "the one." Without question, that night proved to be the best last first date I've ever experienced.

GUEST RECIPE | St. Cecilia Punch

makes 15+ cups

Water, for ring mold

1 to 2 lemons (Meyer if
available)

2 large ripe peaches

2 cups brandy (Calvados or
Applejack is best)

2 cups Appleton Jamaican
rum (other Jamaican
rums will work, permitted
they're not white rum)

1 ripe pineapple

⅔ cup sugar dissolved in ⅓
cup hot water

4 cups strong black tea,
chilled or room tempera-
ture

2 to 3 bottles tart, dry champagne

1 liter seltzer (can substitute
ginger ale; if so, omit the
sugar syrup above)

EQUIPMENT

Punch bowl, ring mold, and
festive cups or glasses (see
Note)

*Sarah Bloom and I met in our early twenties. We were both living in Wash-
ington, D.C., at the time, and she was longtime friends with a guy I briefly
dated. Sarah went on to become a college professor and is now on faculty at
the University of South Florida. When I mentioned I was writing a beverage book, she immediately offered her recipe for St. Cecilia Punch. Named
after a famous eighteenth-century Charleston, South Carolina, social club,
the punch includes tea, pineapple, lemons, liquor, and sparkling wine.
With a combination like that, good times are bound to ensue!*

Fill a ring mold with water and place in the freezer. Slice the lemons,
and cut the peaches into wedges and place in a bowl. Pour the brandy
and rum over the peaches, and refrigerate for 6 to 8 hours. Transfer the
soaked fruit and its liquor to a punch bowl.

Peel, core, and slice the pineapple. Cut the slices into thirds, and add
to the punch bowl. Add the sugar water and tea (omit the sugar water if
using ginger ale instead of seltzer). Stir to fully combine.

Before serving, add the champagne and seltzer and place the ice ring
in the bowl. If having trouble removing the ice from the ring mold, run
it under hot water for a few seconds.

Note: If you don't own a punch bowl, never fear! They're often readily
available at thrift stores or yard sales, often for quite low prices. Otherwise, simply appropriate an existing bowl you already own, such as a
large glass or ceramic bowl. It likely won't have as large of a volume as a
traditional punch bowl, so it'll require more frequent refilling, but it'll
do in a pinch!

Caramelized Apple Cider Punch

Who doesn't love a caramel apple? All of that gooey, oozing goodness coupled with the crisp crunch of apple. It's the stuff of dreams, friends. Add in a kiss of smokiness, courtesy of caramelized simple syrup, a bit of fresh cider, and some brandy, and you've got a grown-up, liquefied version of everyone's favorite autumnal treat.

Begin by making the Caramelized Simple Syrup. Bring 2 cups of water to a boil. Set aside. Meanwhile, mix the sugar with 2 tablespoons of water in a medium-size saucepan. Stir until the mixture resembles the consistency of wet sand. Heat the mixture over medium low, until it turns to a copper penny color. Wait to stir the mixture until the color begins to change, then gently stir it with a metal spoon.

Add the 2 cups of boiled water. Cook until all of the sugar is melted back into the water. Don't worry if the mixture hardens up at first; as it warms up it'll return to a liquid state. Take the pot off the heat, and set aside to cool.

Add the apple cider, brandy, and Carmelized Simple Syrup to a punch bowl. Stir gently. Grate some fresh nutmeg over it, then add the apple slices. Add in seltzer right at serving time. Serve at room temperature or chilled.

makes 16+ cups

8 cups apple cider

3 cups brandy

1 cup Caramelized Simple Syrup (recipe follows)

Freshly grated nutmeg, to taste

1 thinly sliced apple, to serve

1 liter seltzer water, to serve

For the Caramelized Simple Syrup

2 cups + 2 tablespoons water, divided

1 cup sugar

Equipment

Punch bowl and festive cups or glasses

Grapefruit and Rosemary Gin and Tonic Punch

makes 18 cups

- - - - - - - - - - - - - - - -

8 cups grapefruit juice

3 cups gin

1 cup vermouth

1 liter tonic water

Rosemary Simple Syrup
    (recipe follows)

Rosemary-sprig ice ring, to
    serve (see Note)

FOR THE ROSEMARY SIMPLE
SYRUP

1 cup water

1 cup sugar

Two 6-inch fresh rosemary
    sprigs

EQUIPMENT

Punch bowl, ring mold, and
    festive cups or glasses

- - - - - - - - - - - - - - - -

Citrus reaches its peak of ripeness come wintertime. Grapefruits available during the coolest months offer a flavor that far outshines what's available at the grocer's the rest of the year. Here I've cozied up the fresh juice with gin, vermouth, tonic, and rosemary simple syrup. The result is a winter sipper that's equal parts refreshing, herbaceous, and plain old fun.

Begin by making the Rosemary Simple Syrup. Place the water and sugar in a medium-size saucepan. Bring to a gentle simmer, stirring until the sugar has completely dissolved. Add the rosemary sprigs, pressing on them with a spoon to fully submerge them in the sugar water. Remove the pan from the heat, cover with a lid, and leave to infuse for 30 minutes. Strain off the rosemary sprigs, setting aside to compost.

Place the grapefruit juice, gin, vermouth, tonic water, and Rosemary Simple Syrup in a large punch bowl. Stir gently. Add an ice ring (see Note), and serve.

Note: Place several rosemary sprigs and water in a ring mold. Freeze. At serving time, release the ice from the ring mold and place it in the punch bowl.

resources

Buttermilk Starter, Kefir Grains, and Kombucha Starter Cultures
Cultures for Health
www.culturesforhealth.com

Cider, Mead, and Wine-Making Equipment and Supplies (including Airlocks, Bottles, Bottle Cappers, Carboys, Rubber Stoppers, Sanitizers, Siphoning Tubes, and Yeast)
Leeners
www.leeners.com

BSG HandCraft
www.bsghandcraft.com

Dried Herbs
Mountain Rose Herbs
www.mountainroseherbs.com

Rose Water (Organic)
Sweet Essentials NC
www.etsy.com/shop/SweetEssentialsNC

Turbinado Sugar
Wholesome Sweeteners
www.wholesomesweeteners.com

index

about the photographer

Jen Altman is a photographer and writer. Her work has been exhibited throughout North America and is held in private collections across the globe; her clients include Chronicle Books, *Martha Stewart Living, Food & Wine,* and *Kinfolk* magazine among others. Jen is the author of *Instant Love: How to Make Magic and Memories with Polaroids* with Susannah Conway and Amanda Gilligan, *Gem and Stone: Jewels of Earth, Sea and Sky,* and *Photographing Your Children: A Handbook of Style and Instruction.* Jen lives in Asheville, North Carolina, with her three daughters and husband. You can follow her adventures in food and travel at her acclaimed blog, *Nectar.*

about the author

Ashley English has degrees in holistic nutrition and sociology. She has worked over the years with a number of nonprofit organizations committed to social and agricultural issues, is a member of Slow Food USA, and writes a regular column for the quarterly publication *Taproot*. She is the author of four books in The Homemade Living series (*Canning & Preserving, Keeping Chickens, Keeping Bees, Home Dairy*), as well as *A Year of Pies* and *Handmade Gatherings* (Roost Books). Ashley and her family live in Candler, North Carolina, where they are converting their land into a thriving homestead. Follow their adventures at www.smallmeasure .com.